赵彦春

译·注

赵彦春
国学经典
英译系列

英韵 **弟子规**

Canons for Disciples in English Rhyme

王静 绘

高等教育出版社·北京

英韵《弟子规》
中文朗诵

Canons for Disciples
in English Rhyme
English Recitation

总序

由中国先秦史学会国学双语研究分会与高等教育出版社精心策划、精心实施的《百部国学经典英译》系列丛书,适逢我们走进新时代、踏上新征程之际,经过同仁们的共同努力,即将陆续出版发行。这对传播中华优秀传统文化,促进中西文明交流互鉴,具有重要的历史意义和积极的现实意义。

众所周知,我们为中华民族所拥有的五千多年的辉煌文明历史而倍感骄傲和自豪,它支撑着中华民族特有的凝心和聚力,从而使中华民族更坚定地由文化自信走向文化自觉,再到文化自强。

迈向近代以来,随着欧洲所谓的地理大发现,中西文化得以交流。以欧洲为中心的西方文化和以中国为主导的东方文化,几经接触、几经碰撞,两大文化系统需要互相理解、互相认知,于是应运产生了几种学问。在欧洲产生了后来所谓的汉学,在中国产生了后来所谓的西学,同时,与西学相区别,又产生了所谓的中学，也就是后来所谓的国学。

我们从中可以清楚地看到，每当我们中国历史重要转折的关头，一定会出现中学和西学或者说国学和西学问题的大讨论、大辩争。萌芽于明清之际，继之于清代中叶，特别是晚清到民初、到五四运动的东西文化之争，乃至于我们今天持续的国学热，无不是时代的呼唤，无不是历史的需求。在我们中华民族伟大复兴的征程上，重新认识我们的历史，重新认识我们的文化，不仅仅是物质方面的需求，更是精神方面的需求。在我们的文化走向世界之际，我们必须认识自己的优秀传统文化。

那么，什么是国学呢？简单地说，国学也就是中学，也就是中国固有的传统文化。如何学习国学？如何继承国学？我们觉得，应当抓住它最核心的部分、最优秀的部分。也就是说，从整个历史的潮流、历史的过程来看，国学的主流肯定是儒学，它所占的比例最大，影响最深，历史也最为久远。当然，儒学的核心肯定是经学，这不是一个价值判断，而是一个事实判断。我们今天要认识国学，要进一步阐扬国学里面的优秀传统文化，就一定要对中国传统文化的儒学，特别是儒学经典，也包括中国古代一些其他的经典，有重新的认识和重新的诠释。这一点，近年很多学者都讲过了。

其实，我们从历史上看，对于过去的文化重新认识和继承，一定要依赖于对经典的重新发现和重新诠释。比如大家常说的文艺复兴时期，希腊、罗马时代的一些经典性的著作，有不少是重新发现、重新审读、重新注释，甚至是从阿拉伯世界等地方发现和介绍回来的。与希腊、罗马时代的情况有所不同，古代埃及文明的阐扬和解释则是依靠考古发现，比如著名的罗塞塔石解读，包括希伯来的文明也是一样，死海文书的发现，改变了基督教史的一些根本认识。我们中国的例子，历史上已经有过实例，不过也有所不同。

现在，我们正处于一个大发现的时代。改革开放四十年来，国家夏商周断代工程的成功实施，中华文明探源工程的持续开展，极大地推动了中国古代文明研究并取得了丰硕的学术成果。特别是20世纪末郭店简、上博简，包括21世纪初清华简等等的发现与研究，为重新审视、重新诠释我们的国学经典，创造了良好的条件，奠定了可靠的基础。

中国的国学这样博大，我们主要认识什么呢？我们认为，还是那些经典的、最有影响、起最根本作用的一些文献。

毫无疑问，让世界了解国学的最佳途径是国学的翻译。高等教育出版社出版的这套图书以还原中华文化为旨归，以诗译诗，以经译经，向世界展现原作的文辞之美和思想境界。因其翻译思想和方法上的突破，可以说这套书就是用英语撰写的原著。

衷心期待《百部国学经典英译》系列丛书早日面世。

李学勤

2018年7月1日于北京

Introduction

A Hundred Chinese Classics in English, initiated and implemented by Chinese Classics Bilinguals' Association and Higher Education Press, is coming out at the right time we enter a new era and embark on a new journey. It is of great historical and practical significance to introduce the best of traditional Chinese culture to the world and promote the exchange and mutual learning between Chinese and Western civilizations. The efforts and achievements are worth our congratulations.

As we all know, the Chinese nation has a civilization that has been shining with great splendor for more than five thousand years, which gives Chinese people an unparalleled pride while reinforcing the unique coagulant and cohesive might of the nation and propelling the nation from self-confidence to self-awareness and then to self-development.

Since the dawning of modern times, with the so-called geographical discoveries in Europe, cultural exchanges between China and the Western countries have been on the way.

Eurocentric Western civilization and the oriental civilization led by China that have gone through all shocks, conflicts and clashes, need to understand and recognize each other. In due course, several kinds of learning have emerged. The so-called Sinology came about in Europe, and the so-called Western learning came to be in China. At the same time, different from Western learning, the so-called Chinese learning (Chinese classics in particular) came on the stage.

It can be clearly seen that there must be great discussions or debates between Chinese learning and Western learning, or sinology and Chinese classics at every important turning point in Chinese history. The contention between Western and Eastern cultures that sprouted in the Ming and Qing dynasties, continued in the middle of the Qing dynasty, and surged from the late Qing dynasty to the early Republic of China and the May 4th Movement, and even today's continuous craze for Chinese classics can all be seen as the call of times and the need of history. On the journey of Chinese rejuvenation, it is a necessity, not only materially but also spiritually, to recognize our history and culture again. As our culture is going out to the world, we must know our own culture and tradition.

Then, what is Chinese classics as a subject? Generally speaking, Chinese classics is Chinese learning, that is, the traditional Chinese culture. How to study Chinese classics and how to carry it on? We believe that the most crucial and the best part should be seized. In other words, from the trend and process of history, the mainstream of Chinese classics should be Confucianism, which has the largest proportion, the deepest influence and the longest history. Of course, the core of Confucianism must be Confucian classics, which is a judgment of facts rather than values. In today's world, we need to have a new understanding and reinterpretation of traditional Chinese Confucianism, especially the Confucian classics and some other classics, in order to know traditional Chinese culture and its quintessence. It is a point that many scholars have mentioned in recent years.

In fact, from a historical point of view, recognition and inheritance of a past culture must rely on the rediscovery and reinterpretation of classics. For example, in the Renaissance, some classics in Greece and Rome were rediscovered, reexamined, reannotated, or even found and introduced back from Arabia and other places. Different from the times in Greece and Rome, the exposition and interpretation of ancient civilization in Egypt relied on archaeological discoveries such as the famous Rosetta Stone Deciphering. The same is true of Hebrew civilization. The discovery of Dead Sea Scrolls has changed some fundamental understandings of the history of Christianity. China also had some examples in history, somewhat different though.

We are now in an age of great discovery. Since the reform and opening up forty years ago, with the successful implementation of the national Xia-Shang-Zhou chronology project, the sustainable development of the Exploration of the Source of Chinese Civilization Project has greatly promoted the academic achievements of ancient civilization in China. In particular, at the end of the 20th century, the discoveries and study of Guodian Bamboo Slips, Shangbo Bamboo Slips, including Tsinghua Bamboo Slips at the beginning of the 21st century, have laid a good foundation for a re-examination and reinterpretation of Chinese classics.

Chinese classics is so extensive and profound. What should we mainly know about it? We believe it is the most classic, the most influential and the most fundamental literature that we must get to know.

Without doubt, the best way for the world to know Chinese classics is through their translations. This series of books published by Higher Education Press, aimed at rendering Chinese culture as it is, that is, translating Poesie into Poesie and Classic into Classic, will show the world the charm and profundity of the originals. These translations can be regarded as "originals" in English because of the epistemological and methodological innovations embodied therein.

I'm sincerely looking forward to the coming of *A Hundred Chinese Classics in English*.

Li Xueqin
Beijing, July 1, 2018

Contents 目录

Foreword	1	序
Filiality	13	入则孝
Fraternity	34	出则悌
Good Behavior	50	谨
Faithfulness	74	信
Loving All	96	泛爱众
Being Kind	118	亲仁
Study	125	余力学文
Canons for Disciples (Pinyin Version)	142	附录:《弟子规》全文（汉语拼音版）
Afterword	153	跋

序

为久负盛名者作序,诚惶诚恐自不必说。谦虚的赵彦春教授早就把译稿发给我,景仰与敬畏之情难以言表,而真诚的约请更是难以婉拒。由于学识所限,恐怕难以进行独到的分析和评价,故不揣浅陋,从翻译学习者、译文鉴赏者、译本使用者的角度谈谈我对《英韵〈弟子规〉》的感受。

蒙先师汪榕培先生不弃,入师门学习典籍翻译;却天性愚钝,又诸多懒散,除与先生合译汤显祖的《南柯记》和完成几篇论文外,无他建树。但跟随先生求学的经历培养了我终身学习的热情和能力,也使我对经典译作批评赏析非常感兴趣并对各位译界大家无限仰慕。有些大家因年代、年龄、地理距离,于我如璀璨的星辰挂于天际,熠熠生辉却遥不可及;也有些大家因为同时代的缘故,有如灯盏,闪耀着自己,也照亮着别人,似乎更能让人感受到他们的光芒和温度。

翻译，特别是典籍翻译，绝不单纯是翻译技巧的问题，更需要文化能力、语言能力，甚至是与原作感同身受的移情能力。亲身实践，在做中学，能够有很大的助益，但自己动手翻译之前阅读学习一些经典译作可能要比盲目的、低层次的反复实践更有益一些。

在收到赵彦春教授的译稿之前，其实我已经通过微博、微信公众号等渠道密切关注他的国学典籍译作。又读《英韵〈弟子规〉》，妙译佳句俯拾即是，信手拈来便都朗朗上口。虽是蒙学典籍，看似容易，实则是对译者功底的严格考验。《弟子规》是三字一行，四行形成一个诗节，表达一个完整的意思；隔行押韵，但也偶有AABB韵式，如"财物轻，怨何生？言语忍，忿自泯"一节。《弟子规》和其他蒙学典籍一样，也具有行短句、用韵律、重整齐来表达丰富的思想内容和文化内涵的特点，具有重要的教化作用。若能在翻译中把语言形式、思想内容、文化内涵这三个方面完整地表达出来，做到形神兼备，当是译功了得，而在严格的限定之下潇洒自如地表达又是一个怎样的境界。赵彦春教授的《英韵〈弟子规〉》一如原文，堪当教科书式的译本。

赵教授的译本在我的教学实践中确实是起到了教科书的作用。每年的春季学期我会为本科生开设一门公选课，课程名称就叫"国学经典诵读与英译"。这门课属于通识类课程，学生不限年级和人数，有时选课者多达百人。我们通常从蒙学典籍入手，到史学典籍选篇结束。学生首先是诵读国学典籍，在此基础上比较、选择英译本。

我一般在开学初布置了要学习的篇目以后，让学生自己回去选择译本，在课堂上主要分享、比读、赏析。我鼓励学生有自己的偏好，鼓励他们表达自己的看法。现在的学生如初生牛犊，多了些锐气和勇气，少了些对权威大家的推崇。

就《弟子规》来说，学生找到三个可获得的译本，选择赵彦春教授译本的学生占绝对的比例，学生给出的理由包括三词对三字、形式齐整；用词精到准确；韵律清晰上口；有语内翻译帮助理解，语际翻译帮助提高英语水平；思想表达到位。

翻译是容易引发质疑的存在。比如前面举过的例子"财物轻，怨何生？言语忍，忿自泯"一节，赵教授给出的译文是：

Properties you despise;
No disputes arise.
Harshness you restrain;
None will complain.

学生查字典后指出："怨"字从心，有"怨恨、仇恨"的意思，注重心理感受，未必是"争论"（disputes）。其实能外化表达的仇恨都不严重，最怕郁结于心，终成大患。同样"忿"字从心，"心"指心绪，"分"意为"由一而多"，合起来表示"心绪散乱""心情由一定变成不确定"。忿是怒的初级阶段。那么译文与原文中的"怨何生？"和"忿自泯"自然有所出入。也有的学生指出"财物轻"中的"轻"作为动词是中性词，强调的是"不看重"，并非"视金钱如粪土"，而despise表示"鄙视"，语气太重。

我对学生的讨论向来是鼓励的，虽然质疑臧否大家也会有些心虚，但大学教育所提倡的不就是不畏权威、批判性思维吗？《弟子规》上也说"心有疑，随札记，就人问，求确义"。当然，我也会挑战学生，鼓励他们批评别人翻译的同时，尝试找出或自己给出更好的译文。遗憾的是，到现在还没有人做到。

质疑是学术的开端，但它不构成学术本身。学生的质疑应该向更大的系统拓展。翻译不是译文字而是译文学，更不用说说文解字了。语言是表征的，翻译是两种语言系统之间进行妥协找到最佳的表征。反观赵译的"Properties you despise"，它与"财物轻"竟是铢两悉称，而与下一行的"No disputes arise"也顺接自然，可谓天衣合缝。孤立地看，"despise"和"disputes"与原文的"轻"和"怨"有距离，但组合而产生的函项与原文相比照却是如此的贴切。这正是翻译的神奇之处！我想这也是普通译者与大家的根本区别吧。

写到这，映入脑海的是对翻译研究的一个调侃："Those who can, translate; those who can't, teach translation; those who can't teach translation, teach translation theory." 我虽然偶尔翻译，却不敢声称自己是译者了。我就是那个不翻不研而教的人啊。走下课堂，脑海里一直有一个倔强的念头，想给出一个更逼近原文的译文，以后作为炫耀的资本，说我修正了赵彦春教授的译文。可我终究不能，终究只是一个仰慕者、欣赏者和学习者。

霍跃红

2018年8月1日于大连

Foreword

I have been fidgeting with trepidation at the attempt to write a foreword for a renowned scholar. It is not hard to imagine with what reverence and awe I accepted the task when Professor Zhao Yanchun contacted me for a foreword to *Canons for Disciples in English Rhyme*. So afraid that I am not in a position to offer any presentable analysis or evaluation, I might as well tell how I feel about this book as a reader, admirer and user.

Brought into the field of translating ancient Chinese classics into English by late Professor Wang Rongpei, I developed keen interest in translation of classics and a passion for lifelong learning if nothing else I have published except the cooperated translation of Tang Xianzu's *The Nanke Dream* and several academic papers. In my academic pursuit, I have come to know a great many translators. Some of them twinkle like bright stars in the sky, great but distant due to the differences of time, age and place while some contemporaries shine like lamps, closer, warmer, and shedding lights on those nearby.

To me, translation, especially the translation of Chinese classics into English involves cultural and linguistic competence and even empathy rather than mere language skills. There is some truth in the saying of "In doing we learn". However, one might learn more and faster by getting nutrition from the masterpieces than by doing translation with eyes closed, repeating mistakes unawares.

Professor Zhao Yanchun is such a lamp that casts warm light on others. Already equipped with a good knowledge of his works through platforms such as MicroBlog and WeChat, I read *Canons for Disciples in English Rhyme* with keen interest and great pleasure, which he emailed to me with the request of a foreword. This work is abundant with lines of exquisite translation, which can be chanted metrically and beautifully. Though a book originally produced for school children, the task of translation could never be taken for granted. It's a great challenge to any translator. The source book is featured with four-lined stanzas with three Chinese characters in each line, rhyming every other line only with occasional exceptions of AABB rhyming scheme, for example, "cai wu qing, yuan he sheng? Yan yu ren, fen zi min". Taken as a whole, the book is similar to other books written for children's enlightenment with tidy short rhymed lines rich in didactic function. It would be quite challenging and demanding to reproduce the linguistic features, ideas and rich cultural connotations while taking into consideration both form and content in the translation. It should be an impossible mission to achieve total freedom within strict constraints. Professor Zhao has made it ! And his translation can serve as a textbook of translation.

I am by no means exaggerating the function of his translation in my teaching experience. Every spring semester I will offer undergraduates an optional course of "Reading Chinese Classics and Their English Translations". Meant as a course of liberal art, it sets no limits to the level and number of applicants, taking as many as 100 plus students. We usually start with enlightenment classics for children and wind up with historic classics. Reading comes first, to be followed by comparison and evaluation of translations.

In the first meeting with my students, I will assign a list of classic works to read and ask students to go back and read extensively, choosing their favorite translation version. Instead of doing most of the lecturing myself, I distribute my class time among students who share their learning experiences, doing analysis and promoting the translation they've decided on. I am there to keep the ball rolling and offer some comments. I have never faced the embarrassment of silent classes. With my encouragement, they are very brave in expressing their ideas and challenging academic authorities.

For the book in question, my students have found three translation versions available and a great majority of students have chosen Professor Zhao Yanchun's. Their reasons for making the choice are various, including the formal equivalence of three English words for three Chinese characters, the accurate diction, the rhymed couplets, the helpful paraphrasing or intra-lingual translation, the excellent inter-lingual translation and the complete rendering of original ideas. This does not mean the class goes without different voices. Say the stanza with AABB scheme we mentioned above, which Professor Zhao rendered into

Properties you despise;
No disputes arise.
Harshness you restrain;
None will complain.

Nothing is more controversial than translation. Some of my

students expressed their different opinions about Professor Zhao's translation after consulting dictionaries. For one thing, both words of "yuan (怨)" and "fen (忿)"express the unhappiness, even hatred within, while Professor Zhao used "disputes" and "complain" to express external behavior. For another, the word "qing (轻)"in the source text is a neutral word, meaning "not paying much attention to" while "despise" in the translation is obviously negative, meaning "having a very low opinion of".

Students' different opinions are always encouraged though sometimes I am also afraid of our own naivety or shallowness. However, aren't those the qualities we should foster in students—critical thinking and challenging authorities? We could find support from such lines of "Having a doubt, Mark it out. Ask all those, Who it knows" from the same book. As a matter of fact, I give more encouragement to students to find or come up with a better translation when they criticize others'. Luckily or unluckily, none has been able to produce or present a better version.

Doubting is the beginning of learning though it is not learning itself. I expect students to go further to a broader and a more complicated system. As a matter of fact, translation is not a matter of transcoding words but a matter of representing text or literature, let alone exegesis or etymology. A language is a system of representation and translation is to find the best representation through compromises between two languages. Now a second glance at Zhao's "Properties you despise" finds it a perfect match with the original and a natural flow to cohere with the next line "No disputes arise", a seamless piece of clothing. In isolation, "despise" and "disputes" may not be exactly equivalent with their decontextualized counterparts. However, their composition yields a mystic function, an apt proxy for the original. This is the magic of translation, which distinguishes between a talent and a non-talent.

Right now, a sarcasm occurs to me: "Those who can, translate; those who can't, teach translation; those who can't teach translation, teach translation theory." Do I belong in the third group? But a tenacious idea has haunted me: "A better version?!" How I wish I could produce a better translation so that I can show off to other scholars that I have revised or improved Professor Zhao's work! A futile attempt! After all, I am only an admirer, an appreciator and a learner.

Huo Yuehong
Dalian, August 1, 2018

弟子规，

圣人训。

首孝悌，

次谨信。

Disciples, all ages,
Follow the sages.
Piety comes afore,
Credit, add more.

作为弟子，应遵从圣人的教诲。首先在日常生活中，要做到孝顺父母，友爱兄弟姐妹。其次要小心谨慎，要讲信用。

As a disciple, you should follow the teachings of the sages. In daily life, you should be filial to your parents, fraternal to your siblings, and then you should be careful with everything and be a man of good credit.

泛爱众,
而亲仁。
有余力,
则学文。

The masses above,
Everyone you love.
With more energy,
Further your study.

和大众相处时要平等博爱,并且亲近有仁德的人,向他们学习。如果还有多余的时间和精力,就应该好好地学点有益的学问。

As a member of the society, you should love others, and learn from those with good virtues. If you have more time and energy, you should carry on with your study.

入则孝

Filiality

父母呼,
应勿缓。
父母命,
行勿懒。

When parents call,
Do not stall.
At their demand,
Reply off hand.

父母呼唤，应及时回答，不要慢吞吞的很久才应答。父母有事交代，要立刻动身去做，不可拖延或推辞偷懒。

When your parents call for you, you shouldn't stall, giving your excuses. If they want you to do something, you should reply immediately.

父母教,

须敬听。

父母责,

须顺承。

Should they teach,
Hear their preach.
At their discipline,
Reform you begin.

父母教导我们为人处世的道理,是为了我们好,所以我们应该恭敬地聆听。做错了事,父母责备教诫时,应当虚心接受,不可强词夺理,使父母亲生气、伤心。

We should listen to our parents when they teach us the way of life because they wish us well. And we should accept their discipline if we are wrong. Your retort or excuse will make your parents angry or sad.

冬则温，

夏则清。

晨则省，

昏则定。

A warm winter,
A cool summer.
A diligent morning,
A reposed evening.

侍奉父母要用心体会，要让他们冬暖夏凉。早晨起床之后，应该先探望父母，并向父母请安。下午回家之后，要将今天在外的情形告诉父母，向父母报平安，使老人家放心。

Take care of your parents, keeping them warm in winter and cool in summer. First thing in the morning, you should pay respect to them, and in the evening when you are back home you should report to them so that they can be reposed.

出必告，
反必面。
居有常，
业无变。

Wherever you go,
Let them know.
A living staid,
A career made.

外出离家时，须告诉父母要到哪里去，回家后还要当面禀报父母，让父母安心。平时起居作息，要有规律，做事有常规，事业上还要有所成就。

When you go out, tell your parents where you are going and let them know when you are back. You should be regular with your living, and try to be successful in your life.

事虽小,
勿擅为。
苟擅为,
子道亏。

Do take care
In any affair.
If you're rash,
You make trash.

纵然是小事,也不要任性,擅自做主,而不向父母禀告;如果任性而为,那便很容易出错,这样有损为人子女的本分。

However trivial a matter may be, you should let your parents know. Don't make bold and take a rash action. In that case, you may make errors, unworthy to be a good son.

物虽小，
勿私藏。
苟私藏，
亲心伤。

Don't you slide;
Nothing you hide.
If you do,
They will rue.

做事情不要偷偷摸摸，不知不觉地染上坏习惯，不论东西有多小都不要把它隐藏起来。如果那样的话，你的品德就有所缺失，父母亲知道了也一定会伤心。

You should not slide or slide into bad habits, nor should you hide anything no matter how small it is. If you do that, you will be morally inadequate, and your parents will feel worried about it.

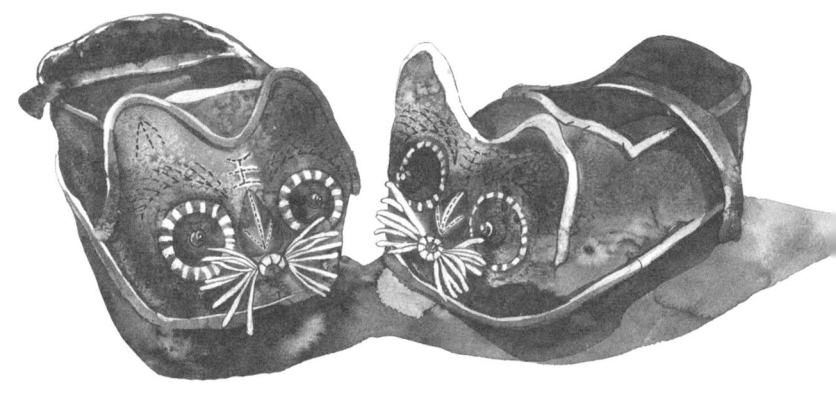

亲所好,

力为具。

亲所恶,

谨为去。

At their request,
Do your best.
What they despise
You do otherwise.

父母亲所喜好的东西,希望你去做,你就应该尽力去执行;父母所厌恶的东西,你要小心谨慎,尽力避开。

> You should try your best to do what your parents want you to do; you should take care and keep away from what they don't like.

身有伤，
贻亲忧。
德有伤，
贻亲羞。

Your health unwell,
They're in hell.
Your worth unraised,
They feel abased.

要爱护自己的身体，不要使身体轻易受到伤害，让父母亲忧虑。要注意自己的品德修养，如果我们做出伤风败德的事，父母亲便会蒙受耻辱。

You should take care of yourselves, not to be injured or fall ill in case your parents are worried. You should pay attention to your virtue. If you do something immoral, your parents will feel shame.

亲爱我,

孝何难?

亲恶我,

孝方贤。

With their care,
Piety's not rare;
If they're picky,
Piety's not easy.

当父母喜爱我们关心我们的时候,孝顺是很容易的事;当父母亲不喜欢我们,或者管教过于严厉的时候,我们也一样孝顺,这就难能可贵了。

When our parents take care of us, it is easy to be filial; when they don't love us or when they are so demanding, your filial piety is the best.

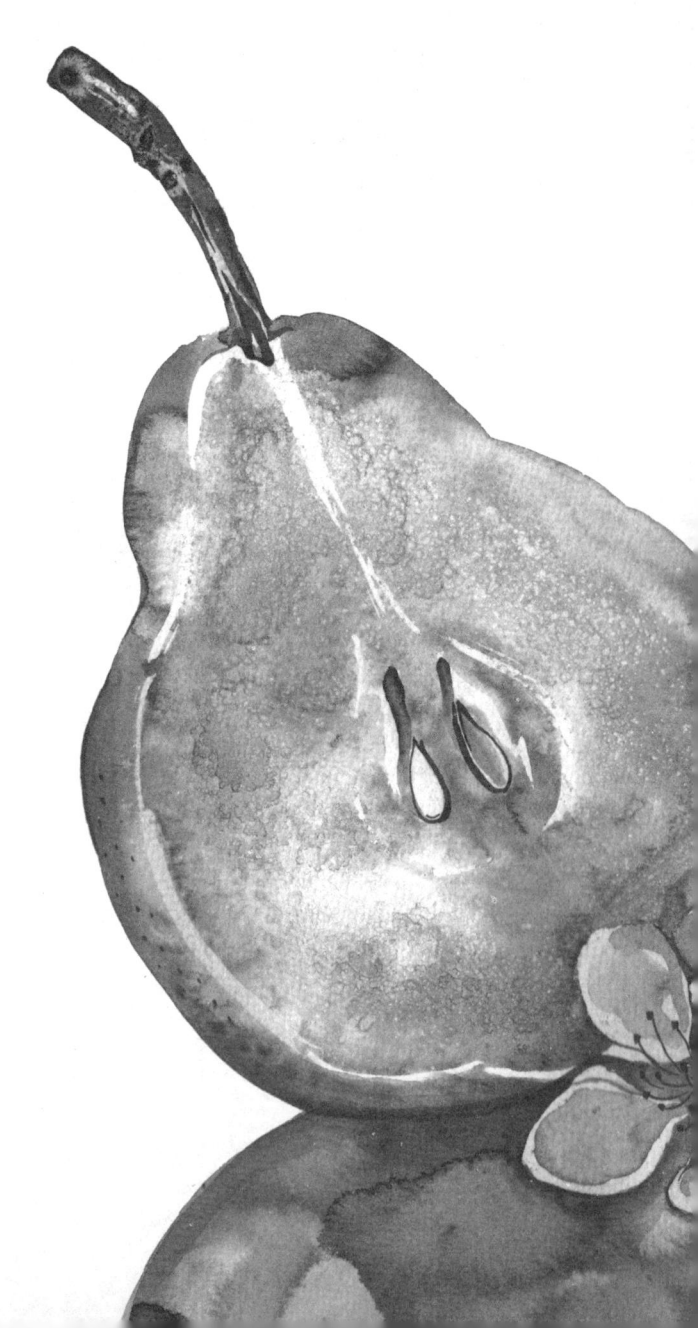

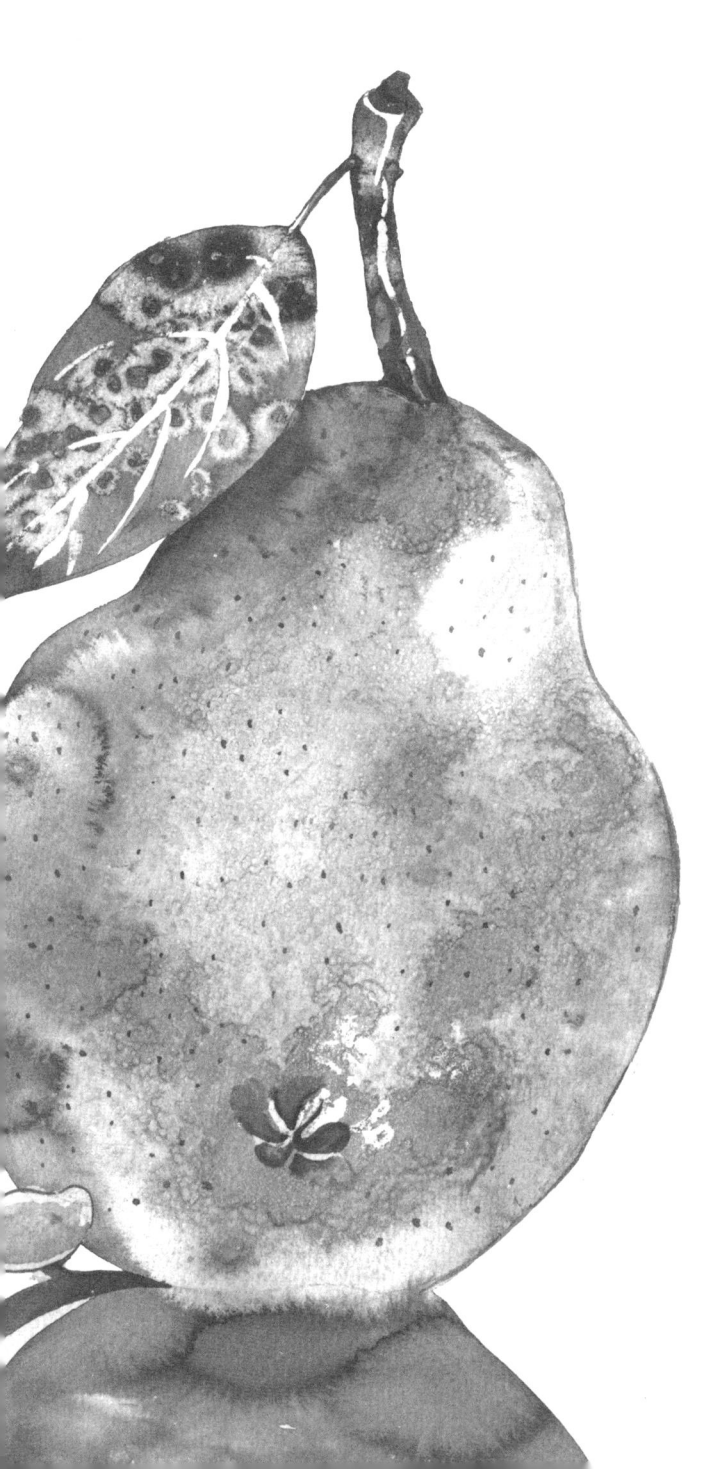

亲有过,
谏使更。
怡吾色,
柔吾声。

Should they sin,
Upon them win!
With smiling eyes,
With no sighs.

父母亲有过错时，应小心劝导，使之改过向善。态度要诚恳，声音要柔和，和颜悦色。如果父母不听规劝，要耐心等待，等父母情绪好转或是高兴的时候，再继续劝导。

If our parents commit errors or sins, we should admonish them, earnestly, gently and smilingly. If they don't listen, we should wait patiently until they feel better.

谏不入,
悦复谏。
号泣随,
挞无怨。

If they protest,
You may obtest.
Again and again,
Do not complain.

如果父母依然不接受,甚至生气,我们也要恳求父母改过,纵然自己遭遇到责打,也无怨无悔,免得父母一错再错,铸成大错。

If they remain unchanged or even get angry, you should still persist in your persuasion. Even if you are blamed or chastised, you should not regret or retreat in case they lapse into the seriousness of mistakes.

亲有疾,
药先尝。
昼夜侍,
不离床。

When they're ill,
Taste their pill.
Day and night,
Never you slight.

当父母亲生病时,子女应当尽心尽力地照顾,一旦病情沉重,就更要昼夜服侍,不可以随便离开。

When your parents are ill, you should take full care of them; when they are seriously ill, you should wait on them day and night, never taking chance to leave them alone.

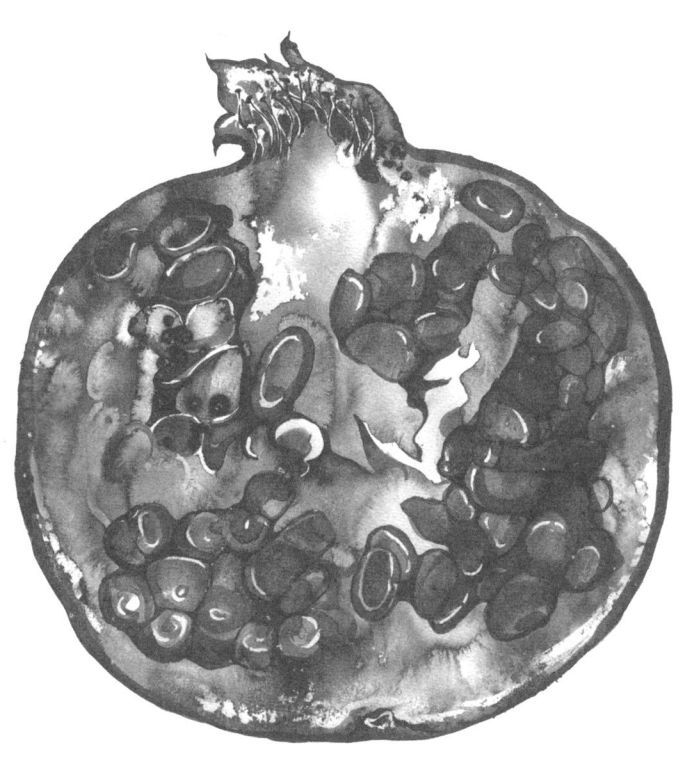

丧三年,

常悲咽。

居处变,

酒肉绝。

Mourning three years,
With saddened tears.
By their tomb,
In cheerless gloom.

父母去世之后,守孝三年,要常常追思、感怀父母教养的恩德。自己的生活起居必须调整改变,不能贪图享受,应该戒绝酒肉。

When your parents pass away, you should observe your mourning for three years, remembering their kindness. You must make changes, living by their tomb, abstaining from meat and wine, and giving up all pleasure.

丧尽礼,

祭尽诚。

事死者,

如事生。

Mourning rites well-run,
Sacrifice properly done.
Serve the deceased,
Reserved the least.

办理父母亲的丧事要合乎礼节,不可草率马虎,也不可以为了面子而铺张浪费,这才是真正的孝顺。祭拜时应诚心诚意,对待已经去世的父母,要如同他们仍然活着一样恭敬。

When preparing your parent's funeral, you should follow the rites, never being careless or extravagant. This is real piety. When you offer sacrifice, you should pay your homage to them as if they were still living.

出则悌

Fraternity

兄道友,
弟道恭。
兄弟睦,
孝在中。

Befriend the elder,
Respect the younger.
Good, good brother,
Love each other.

当哥哥姐姐的要友爱弟弟妹妹,作弟弟妹妹的要懂得恭敬哥哥姐姐,兄弟姐妹能和睦相处,一家人其乐融融,父母自然欢喜,孝道就在其中了。

An elder brother or sister should love his or her younger siblings as if they are good friends; a younger brother or sister should respect his or her elder siblings. If your siblings can love each other and respect each other, your parents will feel happy, hence your filial piety.

财物轻，
怨何生？
言语忍，
忿自泯。

Properties you despise;
No disputes arise.
Harshness you restrain;
None will complain.

与人相处不斤斤计较财物，怨恨就无从生起。注意言语，多说好话，不说坏话，忍住气话，不必要的冲突、怨恨的事情自然消失得无影无踪。

In dealing with people, if you are not selfish, not caring property or money, there will be no ground for hatred; if you pay attention to your speech, using warm words, not harsh ones, and restrain yourself from losing your temper, there will be no confrontation or resentment.

或饮食，
或坐走。
长者先，
幼者后。

For good manner,
All in order.
First the elder,
Then the younger.

良好的生活教育，要从小培养。不论用餐就座或行走，都应该谦虚礼让，长幼有序，让年长者优先，年幼者在后。

A cultivation of good character should start from childhood. When you dine, drink, walk or sit down, you should show your humbleness, taking order, giving priority to elders.

长呼人,
即代叫。
人不在,
己即到。

When elders call,
You answer all.
The called absent,
You'd be present.

长辈有事呼唤人,应代为传呼,如果那个人不在,自己应该主动上前去询问是什么事。可以帮忙就帮忙,不能帮忙时则代为转告。

When an elder calls for somebody, you should answer him in his place, asking what you can do for him. If the one who is needed is absent, you should go ahead to help the elder and if you can't, you may ask him to leave a message.

称尊长，

勿呼名。

对尊长，

勿见能。

Elders, the same,
No their name.
Elders, before you,
Do humble go.

称呼长辈，不可以直呼姓名，在长辈面前要谦虚有礼，不可以炫耀自己的才能。

You may not address an elder directly with his name. Before him you should show your modesty, not to display your talent.

路遇长,

疾趋揖。

长无言,

退恭立。

Elders you greet
Whenever you meet.
If no reply,
You stand by.

路上遇见长辈时,应向前问好,长辈没有事时,即恭敬退后站立一旁,等待长辈离去。

When you meet an elder on the way, you should go ahead to greet him. If he is not engaged with something, you should withdraw with respect and stand aside, waiting for him to leave.

骑下马，
乘下车。
过犹待，
百步余。

They gallop ahead;
You follow instead.
Be properly kind,
Some distance behind.

根据古礼，不论骑马或乘车，你都应该跟在长者的后面，如果长者从后面赶过来，你应该等他离去稍远，约百步之后，才可以离开。

According to the rituals, whether you drive a cart or ride a horse, you should follow your elder. When an elder catches up from behind, you should stop for a while. When he's away, about one hundred steps, you may go on your way.

长者立,
幼勿坐,
长者坐,
命乃坐。

If they stand,
Don't sit, and
If they sit,
Don't follow suit.

与长辈同处,长辈站立时,晚辈应该陪着站立,不可以自行就座,长辈坐定以后,吩咐坐下,我们才可以坐。

When you are with an elder, you should stand if he stands. You may not take a seat. When an elder is seated, you may take a seat at his request.

尊长前，
声要低。
低不闻，
却非宜。

Before your elder,
Your voice lower.
Speaking too low,
Unheard you'll go.

与尊长交谈，声音要柔和适中，回答的声音量太小让人听不清楚，也是不恰当的。

When talking with an elder, you should lower your voice. It is not proper either if you speak too low to be heard.

进必趋,

退必迟。

问起对,

视勿移。

Approach him fast,
And retreat last.
To answer, rise,
Steady your eyes.

有事要尊长帮忙,就快步向前,退回去时,必须稍慢一些才合乎礼节。当长辈问话时,应当专注聆听,眼睛不可以东张西望。

> If you need an elder to help you, you should approach him fast; when you retreat, you should leave slowly. When an elder asks you a question, you should listen carefully, not looking aside.

事诸父,

如事父。

事诸兄,

如事兄。

Serve a father
Like your father;
Serve a brother
Like your brother.

对待叔叔、伯伯等尊长,要如同对待自己的父亲一般孝顺恭敬,对待同族的兄长,要如同对待自己的兄长一样友爱尊敬。

Respect seniors and elders. Treat a father as if he were your own father, and treat a brother as if he were your own brother.

謹

Good Behavior

朝起早，

夜眠迟。

老易至，

惜此时。

Early to rise.
Late, waking eyes.
One ages fast;
Now's turning past.

为人子应早起，把握光阴及时努力。岁月不待人，青春要珍惜。

One should get up early to make full use of time to study. Cherish your time and prime; one ages fast, and now is becoming past.

晨必盥,
兼漱口。
便溺回,
辄净手。

A morning bath,
A cleaned mouth.
At th' toilet stand,
Wash your hand.

养成良好的卫生习惯,才能确保健康。早晨起床后,务必洗脸、刷牙、漱口使精神清爽,有一个好的开始。大小便后,一定要洗手。

To have good health you should pay attention to your personal hygiene. When you get up in the morning, you should wash your face, brush your teeth and rinse your mouth to start your day with a good spirit. After using the toilet, you should wash your hands.

冠必正，
纽必结。
袜与履，
俱紧切。

Being capped right,
And buttoned tight.
Socks and shoes,
Tidy and close.

要注重服装仪容的整齐清洁，帽子要戴端正，衣服扣子要扣好，袜子穿平整，鞋要跟脚。

One should be dressed properly, capped right, buttoned tight, and your socks and shoes should be tidy, close to your feet.

英韵《弟子规》

置冠服，
有定位。
勿乱顿，
致污秽。

Cap and gown.
Up and down.
Keep the order,
Not torn asunder.

回家后衣、帽、鞋袜都要放在固定的位置，避免造成脏乱，要用的时候又要找半天。

When you come back home, your cap and gown and so on should be in their proper places so that you don't have to look for them here and there when you need them.

衣贵洁,

不贵华。

上循分,

下称家。

Keep clothes clean,
Not to preen.
Your proper blouse
Befits your house.

穿衣服需注重整洁,不必讲究是否昂贵华丽是否是名牌。穿着应考量自己的身份及场合,更要衡量家中的经济状况。

Keep your clothes neat and clean. Don't worry about the cost, brand or luxury. You should consider your status and situation. What you need should befit your family budget.

对饮食，
勿拣择。
食适可，
勿过则。

Eat your meal
A proper deal.
Just be temperate
Or stay moderate.

日常饮食要注意营养均衡，多吃蔬菜水果，少吃肉，不要挑食，不可以偏食，避免过量，以免增加身体的负担，危害健康。

You should have a well-balanced diet, eating enough vegetables, fruits, less meat, not picky or particular, or over fed, on guard against ill health.

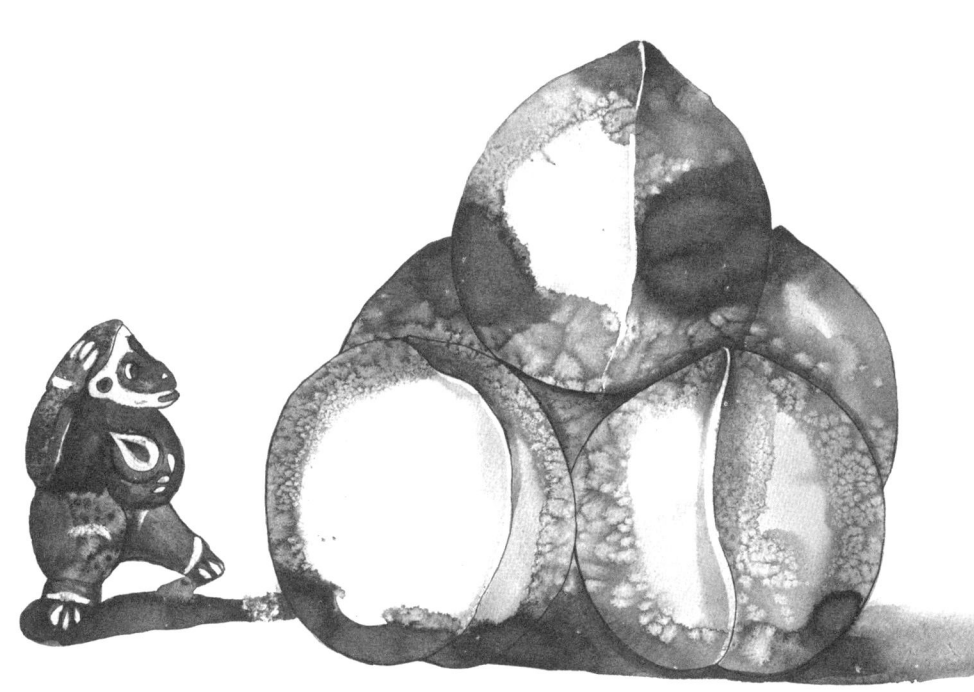

英韵《弟子规》

年方少，

勿饮酒。

饮酒醉，

最为丑。

You, youth fine,
Drink no wine.
If you're drunk,
You're a junk!

饮酒有害健康，要守法，青少年未成年不可以饮酒。成年人饮酒也不要过量，试看醉汉疯言疯语，丑态毕露，惹出多少是非！

Drinking is harmful to health. A youth should be law-biding, drinking no spirit. An adult should not drink too much. Look at those drunkards, how mad and ugly they are! What trouble they make!

步从容，
立端正。
揖深圆，
拜恭敬。

An easy pace,
A forward face.
A deep bow,
With respect enow.

走路时步伐应从容稳重，不慌不忙，不急不缓。站立时要端正站相，抬头挺胸，精神饱满，不可以弯腰驼背，垂头丧气。问候他人时，不论鞠躬或拱手都要真诚恭敬，不能敷衍了事。

You should walk at an easy pace, not hurried; you stand erect, chest held up and well-spirited, not hunching or looking dejected. When greeting others, bowing or cupping your hands, you should show enough respect, with no messing.

勿践阈，

勿跛倚。

勿箕踞，

勿摇髀。

Do not falter;
Do not totter.
Do not splay;
Do not sway.

进门时脚不要踩在门槛上，站立时身体也不要站得歪歪斜斜的。坐的时候不可以伸出两腿，腿更不可以抖动，这些都是很轻浮、傲慢的举动，有失君子风范。

Do not step on a threshold to falter, do not totter when you need to stand, do not splay out your feet and sway. Such habits are not regarded as good manners.

缓揭帘,

勿有声。

宽转弯,

勿触棱。

Keep your poise;
Make no noise.
Carefully you wend;
No edges offend.

进入房间时,揭帘子、开窗户的动作都要轻一点、慢一点,避免发出声音。在室内活动时,应小心不要撞到物品的棱角,以免受伤。

When you enter a room, either drawing the curtain or opening the window, you should keep your poise and make no noise. When you move in the room you should not touch any edges in case you are hurt.

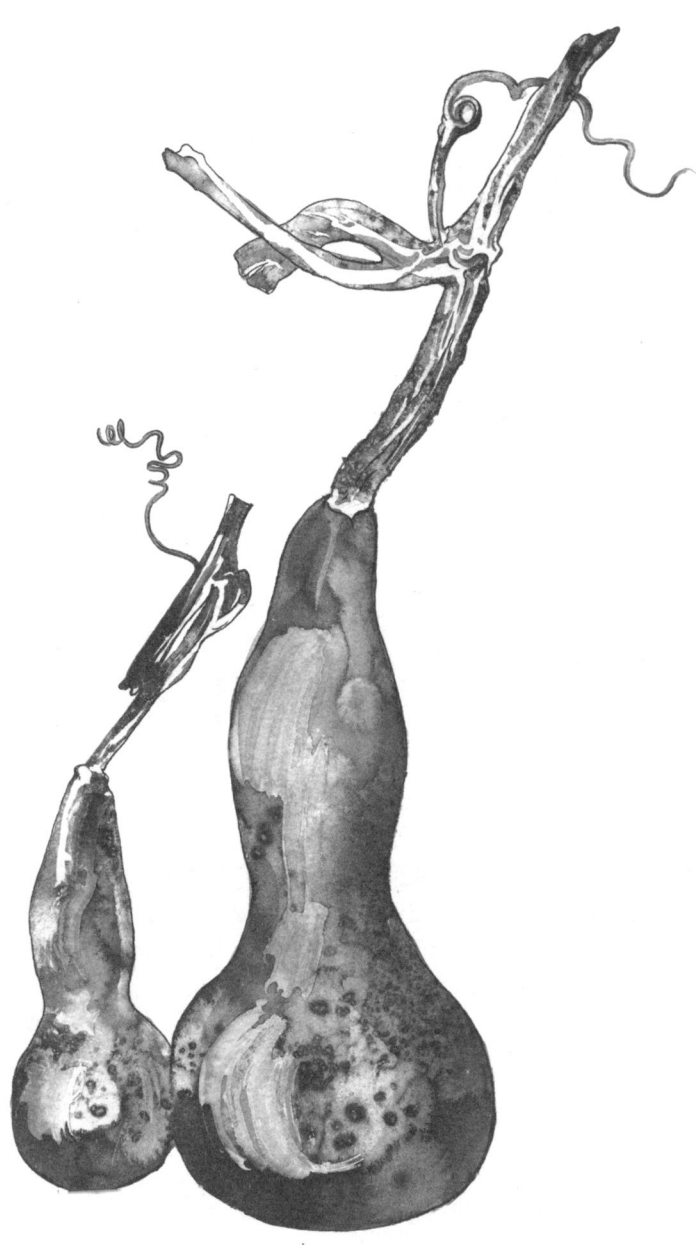

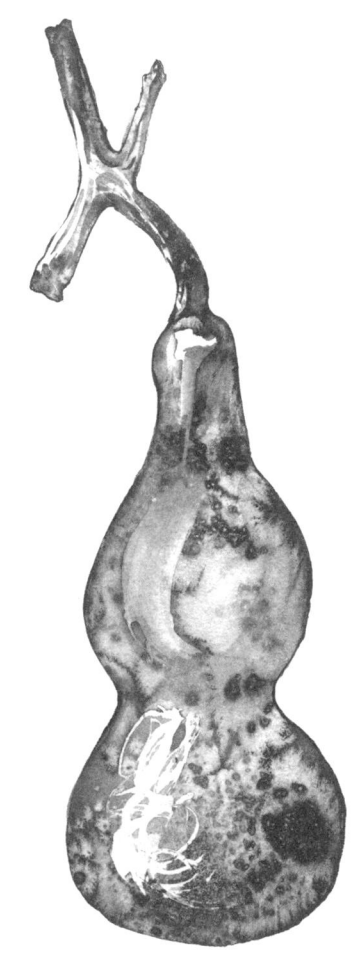

执虚器，

如执盈。

入虚室，

如有人。

Take the pot,
Careful a lot.
Enter the room
Like a groom.

拿东西时要注意，即使是拿着空的器皿，也要像里面装满东西一样，小心谨慎以防跌倒或打破。进入无人的房间，也要像有人在一样，不可以随便。

You should be careful when you take or hold something. Even if a vessel is empty, you should hold it as if it is full in case you fall or break it. When you enter an empty room, you should not make bold, as if your bride is there.

事勿忙,

忙多错。

勿畏难,

勿轻略。

More you haste,
More you waste.
Fear no nut,
Neglect no butt.

做事不要急急忙忙、慌慌张张,因为忙中容易出错,不要畏苦怕难而犹豫退缩,也不可以草率,随便应付了事。

Do not make haste or hurry when you do something because you may make mistakes in that way. You should not hesitate or cringe when doing something difficult, nor should you be negligent, taking no heed of details.

斗闹场，
绝勿近。
邪僻事，
绝勿问。

From the bray
Do keep away.
From what's profane
Do yourself restrain.

凡是容易发生争吵打斗的不良场所，如赌博、色情等是非之地，要勇于拒绝，不要接近，以免受到不良影响。一些邪恶下流，荒诞不经的事也要谢绝，不听、不看，不要好奇地去追问，以免污染了善良的心性。

You should not go to any place where there may be a bray, such as casinos and brothels. If asked to go there, you should decline, not to be adversely affected. And you should restrain yourself from anything that is profane, do not listen, do not look, do not ask in case your good nature is contaminated.

将入门,
问孰存。
将上堂,
声必扬。

Ask who's in,
Before going in.
You loudly call,
Entering the hall.

入门之前,应先问:"有人在吗?"不要冒冒失失就跑进去。进入客厅之前,应先提高声音,让屋内的人知道有人来了。

When entering a door, you should ask: "Is there anybody in?" Do not go inside presumptuously. When entering the hall, you should raise your voice so that you can be heard.

人问谁,
对以名。
吾与我,
不分明。

Asked who came,
Give your name.
If just "me",
That shouldn't be.

如果屋里有人问:"是谁呀?"应该回答自己的名子,而不是"我!我!"让人无法分辨到底是谁。

If you are asked: "Who is there?" you should give your name, not just "It's me!", which may confuse the host.

用人物，

须明求。

倘不问，

即为偷。

If needing some,
A borrower become.
Without the deal,
You're to steal.

借用别人的物品，一定要事先讲明，请求允许。如果没有事先征求同意，擅自取用就是偷窃的行为。

If you need to use something of another person, you must have his permission with a good reason. If you do without his permission, it is an act of theft.

借人物，

及时还。

人借物，

有勿悭。

Return in time
Your borrowed dime.
Others in need,
You help indeed.

借用的物品，要爱惜使用，并准时归还，以后若有急用，再借就不难。人家向你借东西，你如果正好有这样东西，不要因为吝惜而不借给人家。

The borrowed article you should use with care and return in time. It will not be difficult when you need to borrow something from him again. When others need your help, you should help them as much as you can.

信

Faithfulness

凡出言，
信为先。
诈与妄，
奚可焉！

What one saith,
Is his faith.
Craft or art
Plays no part.

开口说话，诚信为先，答应他人的事情，一定要遵守承诺，没有能力做到的事不能随便答应，至于欺骗或花言巧语，更不可为。

When you talk, credit is of first importance. You should keep your promise if you have promised others. You should never make a promise if you are unable to fulfill it. Craft or cheat is what you should avoid in the first place.

话说多，
不如少。
惟其是，
勿佞巧。

Saying too much,
You lose such.
Be as wise,
Away from vice.

话多不如话少，话少不如话好。说话要恰到好处，该说的就说，不该说的绝对不说，立身处世应该谨言慎行，谈话内容要实事求是。

It is better to talk less than talk more; it is better to talk better than talk less. Stop at the right time. Say what you need say, what you don't need you never say. Be careful with your words and deeds. If you must say something, say it as it is.

奸巧语，

秽污词。

市井气，

切戒之。

A glib tongue,
An unfaithful one.
The worldly dust
Evade you must.

不要花言巧语，好听却靠不住。奸诈取巧的言语，下流肮脏的话，以及街头无赖粗俗的口气，都要避免不去沾染。

Do not use flowery words, which are pleasant but not creditable. Try to avoid a glib tongue, dirty words and vulgar slangs.

见未真，
勿轻言。
知未的，
勿轻传。

What is untrue
You don't do.
What's wrongly said
You don't spread.

任何事情在没有看到真相之前，不要轻易发表意见，对事情了解的不够清楚明白时，不可以任意传播，以免造成不良后果。

Don't give your opinion rashly before you see the fact yourself; don't spread something if you don't know it clearly enough.

事非宜，
勿轻诺。
苟轻诺，
进退错。

What is amiss
Do not promise.
If you do,
You'll soon rue.

不合义理的事，不要轻易答应，如果轻易允诺，会造成做也不是，不做也不好，使自己进退两难。

> You shouldn't promise what is not right. If you do that, you will soon rue because of the dilemma: fulfilling it you are wrong; not fulfilling it you are wrong.

凡道字，

重且舒。

勿急疾，

勿模糊。

Whatever you say,
Words you weigh.
There's no hurry;
Never be fuzzy.

讲话时吐字应该清楚，慢慢地讲，不要太快，更不要模糊不清。

When you say something, you should be careful with your words. Never should you hurry. Speak clearly and avoid fuzziness.

彼说长，
此说短。
不关己，
莫闲管。

Lo, that chatter;
Hark, that clatter.
From such nonce
Go at once.

遇到他人来说是非，听听就算了，要有智慧判断，不要受影响，不要介入是非，事不关己不必多管。

When you hear somebody tittle-tattle, you should not be influenced by it, use your brain and keep away.

见人善，

即思齐。

纵去远，

以渐跻。

Seeing someone good,
Discard what's crude.
Though he's afar,
He's your star.

看见他人的优点或善行义举，要立刻想到向他学习、看齐，纵然目前能力相差很多，也要下定决心，逐渐赶上。或者说，他就是照亮你行程的星星。

Seeing someone good or doing good, you should learn from him; though you are far away from him, you should catch up with him. Or rather, he is your star that you can judge your course by.

见人恶,
即内省。
有则改,
无加警。

Seeing someone mean
You should ween.
Undo what's misdone;
Improve what's won.

看见别人的缺点或不良的行为,要反躬自省,检讨自己是否也有这些缺失,有则改之,无则加勉。

You should take a look at yourself when you see others' mistakes or misdeeds, and see if you have the like. If you do, you change; if you don't, you better.

唯德学,
唯才艺,
不如人,
当自砺。

For higher grade,
For better trade,
You learn well,
Never to fail.

每一个人都应当重视自己的品德、学问和才能技艺的培养,如果感觉到有不如人的地方,应当自我惕励、奋发图强。

Everybody should stress on the cultivation of his morality, learning and performance. If you don't find yourself someone's equal, you should cheer up and catch up.

若衣服,
若饮食,
不如人,
勿生戚。

To wear fine,
Or to dine,
Don't you care,
And worry ne'er.

至于外表穿着,或者饮食不如他人,则不必放在心上,更没有必要忧虑自卑。

If you are not his equal in clothing and eating, you don't have to care or feel inferior.

闻过怒,

闻誉乐,

损友来,

益友却。

Angry when abased,
Happy when praised,
You've real friend?
That's the end!

如果一个人听到别人说自己的缺点就生气,听到别人称赞自己就欢喜,那么坏朋友就会来接近你,真正的良朋益友反而逐渐疏远退却了。

If you feel angry when hearing somebody mentioning your shortcomings and pleased when praised, you will have no real friend. Bad people will come to you and your good friends will go away.

闻誉恐,

闻过欣,

直谅士,

渐相亲。

Abashed when praised,
Glad when abased.
Your good friend
Comes to depend!

反之,如果听到他人的称赞而局促不安,当别人批评自己的缺点时,不但不生气,还能欢喜接受,那么正直诚信的人,就会渐渐喜欢和你近亲而信任你了。

On the contrary, if you feel abashed when others praise you and glad when you are abased with criticisms, you will have good friends. They will come to you and depend on you.

无心非,

名为错。

有心非,

名为恶。

A careless make
Is a mistake.
With enough heed,
It's a misdeed.

无心之过称为错,若是明知故犯,有意犯错便是恶行。

What you have done out of carelessness is a mistake. If you do it with enough heed, it is a misdeed.

过能改,
归于无。
倘掩饰,
增一辜。

If feeling shame,
You've no blame.
Trying to hide,
You're spurned aside.

知错能改,是勇者的行为,错误自然慢慢地减少消失,如果死不认错,还要去掩饰,那就是错上加错了。

If you feel shame when realizing you have made a mistake, it is a brave act, and you will bear no blame; if you try to hide your mistake without making an apology, that is a serious misdeed, and you will be spurned aside.

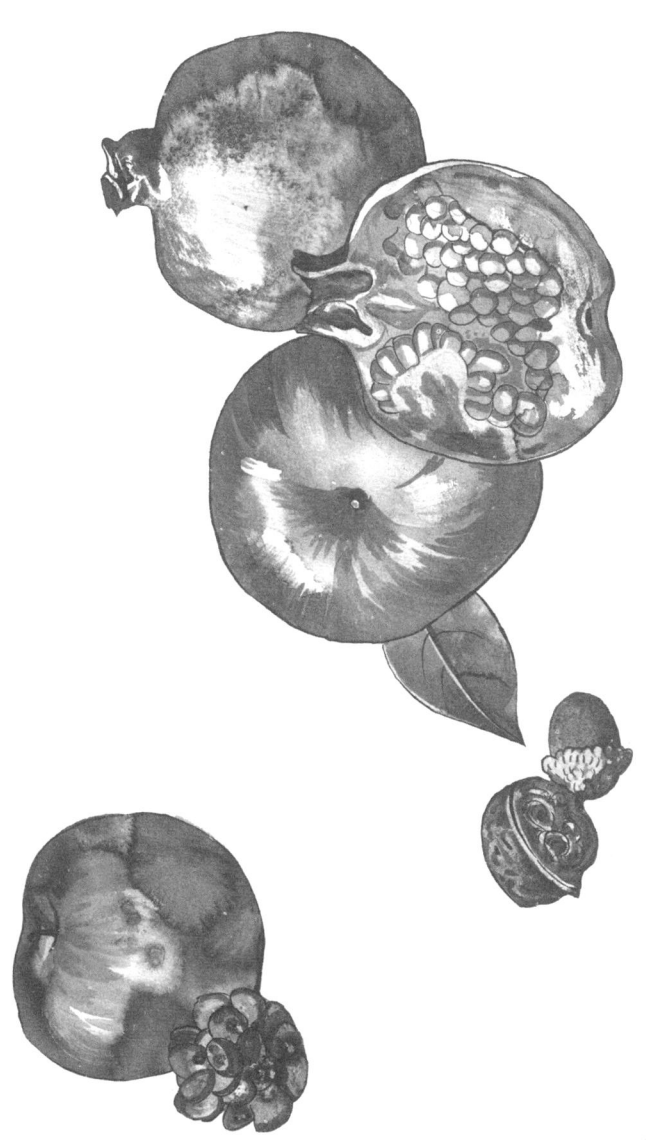

泛爱众

Loving All

凡是人,
皆须爱。
天同覆,
地同载。

Love every one
Under the sun.
The same Nature,
The same creature.

只要是人,就是同类,不分人种和宗教信仰,皆须相亲相爱。同是天地所生万物滋长的,应该不分你我,互助合作,才能维持这个共生共荣的生命共同体。

All men, regardless of creed, race or religion, are of the same kind, and should love each other. Created by the same Nature, they should sustain this community through close cooperation.

行高者，
名自高。
人所重，
非貌高。

A great aim,
A good name.
What one seeks,
Not rosy cheeks.

目标远大之人，名望自然高超。大家所敬重的是他的德行，不是外表容貌。

A man with a great aim will have a very good name. What all respect is his virtue, not his rosy cheeks.

才大者,
望自大。
人所服,
非言大。

Great as such,
Renowned as much.
What is obeyed
Isn't what's said.

有才能的人,处理事情的能力卓越,声望自然不凡,然而人们之所以欣赏佩服,是他的处事能力,而不是因为他很会说大话。

An able man will of course do great things, hence a very good name. However, what people admire is what he does, not what he says.

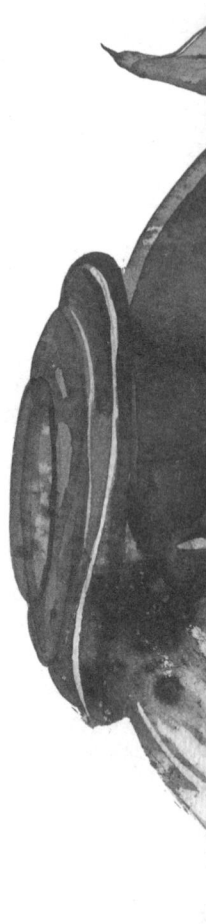
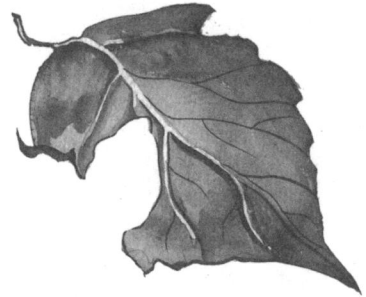

己有能，
勿自私。
人所能，
勿轻訾。

What's your most
You shouldn't boast.
What's others' best
You shouldn't detest.

当你有能力做出成绩的时候，不要自私自利，只考虑到自己，舍不得付出。对于他人的才华，应当学习欣赏赞叹，而不是批评、嫉妒、毁谤。

When you are able and have achieved your most, you shouldn't be selfish or self-centered; you should share what you have with others. And others' talents and achievements you should appreciate, not just criticisms, jealousies and detestation.

勿谄富,

勿骄贫。

勿厌故,

勿喜新。

The rich entertain;
The poor sustain.
The old cherish;
The new nourish.

不要去讨好巴结富人,但可以正常交往,不要在穷人面前骄傲自大,或者轻视他们而要尽量帮助他们。不要喜新厌旧,对于老朋友要珍惜,不要贪恋新朋友或新事物。

Don't flatter the rich but entertain them, don't pride yourself before the poor, nor belittle them but sustain them. Don't abandon the old for the new. Cherish your old friends. Don't be biased towards new friends or new things.

人不闲，

勿事搅。

人不安，

勿话扰。

Don't you bother
The busy other.
Don't you molest
Him who's depressed.

对于正在忙碌的人，不要去打扰他；当别人心情不好，情绪低落的时候，不要闲言闲语干扰他，增加他的烦恼与不安。

Don't bother somebody if he is busy; if he is depressed, don't molest him with prattles in case he is more annoyed or fretted.

人有短，
切莫揭。
人有私，
切莫说。

What's one's defect
Don't you correct.
What others lose,
Don't you disclose.

别人的缺点，不要去揭穿，去指正，对于他人的隐私，切记不要去张扬。

Don't try to expose or correct one's defect; don't disclose others' failure or privacy.

道人善，
即是善。
人知之，
愈思勉。

Saying others good,
You are good.
In high regard,
He'll work hard.

表扬别人，自己便会得到表扬，赞美他人的善行就是行善。当对方听到你的称赞之后，必定会更加勉励行善。

> Praise others, and you are praised; say others good, and you are good. When the other knows your praise, he will work hard in high regard.

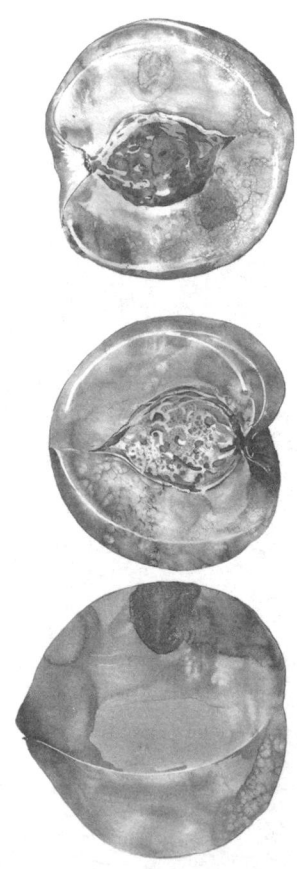

扬人恶,
既是恶。
疾之甚,
祸且作。

Say others bad,
And you're bad.
Someone you despise?
Banes will arise!

张扬他人的过失或缺点,就是做了一件坏事。如果你过于憎恨别人了,你就永远得不到安宁,还会给自己招来灾祸。

Speaking ill of others, you are doing something very bad. If you despise others, you will incur banes.

善相劝,
德皆建。
过不规,
道两亏。

Helping the other,
You both better.
Abetting the other,
You both shatter.

朋友之间应该互相规过劝善,共同建立良好的品德修养。如果有错不能互相规劝,两个人的品德都会有缺陷。

As friends you should help each other, and in this case you both make progress. If you abet each other when going astray, you both shatter.

凡取与,
贵分晓。
与宜多,
取宜少。

Take and give,
Well you live.
Take as such;
Give as much.

财物的取得与给予,一定要分辨清楚明白,宁可多给别人,自己少拿一些,根据需要来索取,按照要求来施与,才能广结善缘,与人和睦相处。

One should have a clear idea of taking and giving. You'd better give others more and take less from them. That is to say, take such an amount as you need it, and give as much as one requires. In this case, you can live well in a harmonious community.

将加人，
先问己。
己不欲，
即速已。

Do unto others
To help others.
What you hate
You should negate.

将事情加到别人身上之前，先要反省，问问自己：换做是我，喜欢不喜欢，如果连自己都不喜欢，就要立刻停止。

When you do something to others, you should have an introspection, asking yourself: Do I like it if I am in his position? If you don't like it, you should stop it immediately.

恩欲报，
怨欲忘。
报怨短，
报恩长。

Remember the bliss,
Forget what's amiss.
The bliss lasts;
What's amiss blasts.

要记住自己的恩惠，时时想着报答，把恼人的糟心事儿都忘掉。愿恩惠常在，怨恨烟消云散。

You should remember your bliss and feel grateful, and you should forget what is amiss that annoys you. May your bliss last and may your resentment disappear.

待婢仆,
身贵端。
虽贵端,
慈而宽。

To your maid,
Dignified and staid.
Staid and dignified,
Kind and magnified.

对待家中的婢女与仆人,要注意自己的品行端正并以身作则,虽然品行端正很重要,但是仁慈宽厚更可贵。

You should be dignified and staid to your maid or servant. Although dignity or staidness is important, you should also be kind and magnified.

势服人，
心不然。
理服人，
方无言。

Shown you power,
None will cower.
Shown your reason,
You win unison.

如果利用仗势强逼别人服从，对方难免口服心不服。唯有以理服人，别人才会心悦诚服，没有怨言。

If you overpower them, they may not be convinced at heart. Only when you show your reason can you win them over.

亲仁

Being Kind

同是人，

类不齐。

流俗众，

仁者稀。

The same kind
Different you find.
Of the multitude,
Few are good.

同样是人，善恶邪正，心智高低却是良莠不齐。跟着世风走的俗人多，仁慈博爱的人少。

Men are of the same kind, but they are different in morality and intelligence. Most of them are vulgar; few of them are good.

果仁者，

人多畏。

言不讳，

色不媚。

Fair who appears
May cause fears.
A righteous one,
He hides none!

如果有仁德的人出现，大家自然敬畏他，因为他是正义的化身，公正无私没有隐瞒，又不刻意去讨好他人。

If a virtuous man appears, most people fear him because he, who may be called fair, is a righteous one, flattering nobody and having nothing to hide.

能亲仁,
无限好。
德日进,
过日少。

Seeking who's kind
Is good, unconfined.
Our worth increases,
Our sin decreases.

能够亲近有仁德的人,向他学习,真是再好不过了,因为他会使我们的德行一天比一天进步,过错也跟着减少。

If we can approach a good person and learn from him, it is good, good without confinement, because everyday our worth increases and our sin decreases.

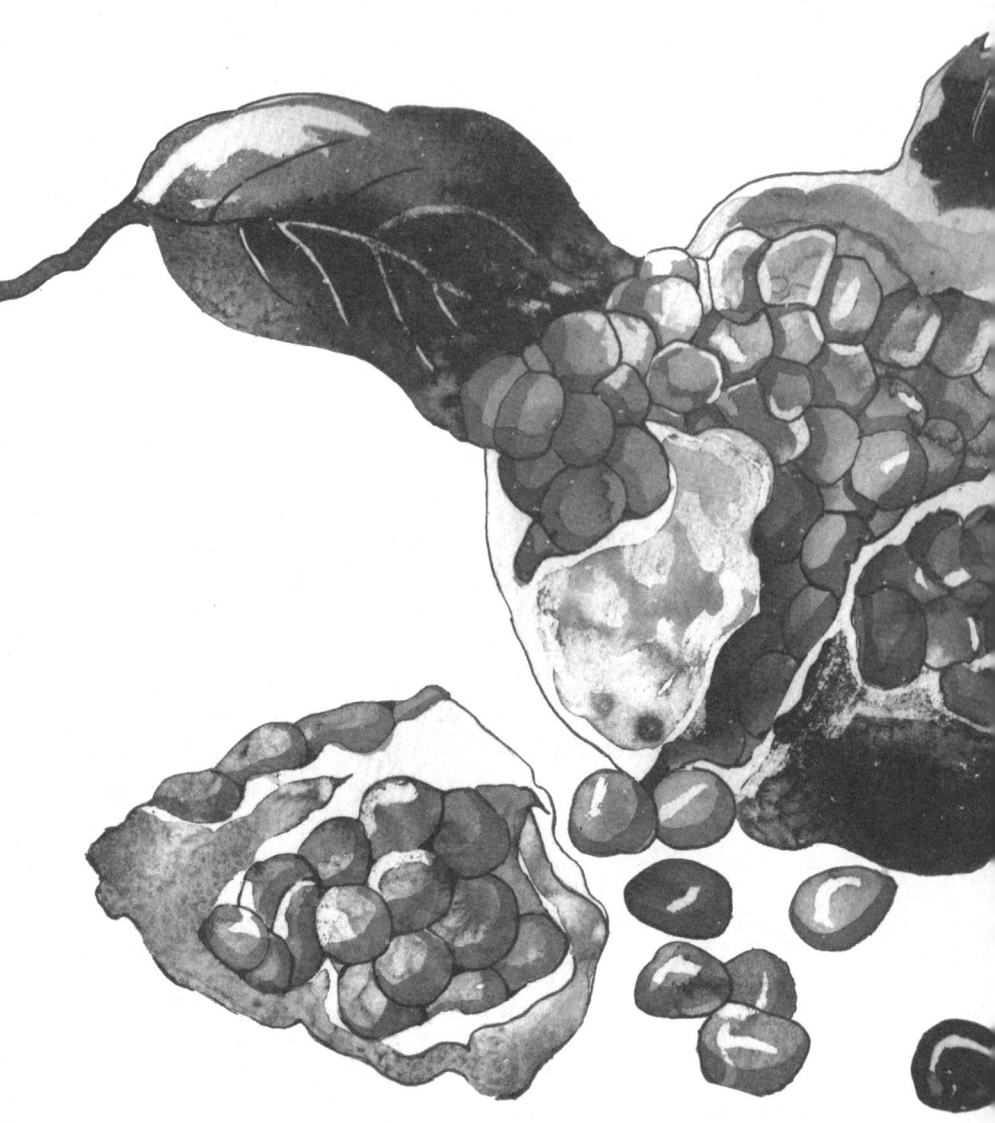

不亲仁,

无限害。

小人进,

百事坏。

Seeking who's unkind
Is harmful, unconfined.
When villains sway;
All go astray.

如果不亲近仁人君子，或只接近不善之人，就会有无穷的祸害，因为不肖的小人会趁虚而入，跑来接近我们，日积月累，我们的言行举止都会受到影响，导致整个人生的失败。

If we don't approach a good person or just seek an unkind one, it is harmful, harmful without confinement, because villains will come into our life. As we are adversely affected, we will go astray from a successful life.

余力学文

Study

不力行，
但学文。
长浮华，
成何人。

With no zest,
You learn lest.
A loafing fop,
Is not tiptop.

若不能身体力行，只知道学习书本知识这样会养成浮华不实的习气，变成一个不切实际的人，如此读书又有何用？

When doing reading, if you do not have enough zest, you can't learn much. You may become a loafing fop, a good-for-nothing. What can be expected of you?

但力行,
不学文。
任己见,
昧理真。

With some zest,
You are unpressed.
A sight bound,
No truth found.

反之,如果只有兴致而不发奋读书,就容易依着自己的偏见做事,发现不了书中包含的真理。

On the other hand, if you have some zest, but do not devote yourself to reading, you will have a limited sight, unable to find truth embodied in the books.

读书法，
有三到。
心眼口，
信皆要。

A good learner,
A good reader.
Eyes, mouth, heart
Play a part.

读书的方法要注重三到：眼到、口到、心到。三者缺一不可，如此方能收到事半功倍的效果。

You should pay full attention to your reading, use your eyes, mouth and heart. These three together are indispensable, ensuring the best effect.

方读此，

勿慕彼。

此未终，

彼勿起。

Reading fixed here,
Nowhere else peer.
If unfinished there,
Nowhere else fare.

读书学习，要专一，这样才能深入，不能才读到这里，就欣羡其他内容而心神不定，必须把这段文字读完，才能读其他内容。

When doing your reading, you should be focused on the line, not peering elsewhere with an unsettled mind. Only when you finish this line can you start the other.

宽为限,
紧用功。
工夫到,
滞塞通。

Use your prime,
Waste no time.
Spare no pain,
Methods you gain.

要充分利用青春年少的大好时光,加紧用功,如果不懈怠偷懒,下足了功夫,原先窒碍不通,困顿疑惑之处自然而然就能迎刃而解了。

You should make full use of your prime and waste no time in learning. If you spare no effort, you will have the key to all puzzles.

心有疑，
随札记。
就人问，
求确义。

Having a doubt,
Mark it out.
Ask all those:
Who it knows?

求学当中，如果心有疑问，应随时笔记，一有机会，就可以向良师益友请教，务必确实明白它的真义。

If you have a doubt when learning, you should take notes so that when you have chance you can ask someone who knows the exact meaning.

房室清，
墙壁净。
几案洁，
笔砚正。

A tidy class-hall,
A clean wall.
Your desk orderly
With good stationery.

书房或学堂要整理清洁，墙壁要保持干净，读书时，书桌上笔墨纸砚等文具要放置整齐，不得凌乱，这样你才能静下心来读书。

Your study or class-hall should be tidy and the wall should be clean, and everything on your desk such as stationery should be in good order. In such condition, you can study well.

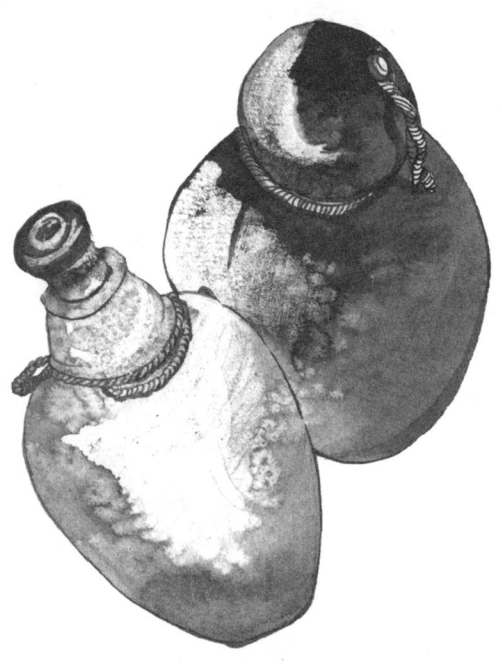

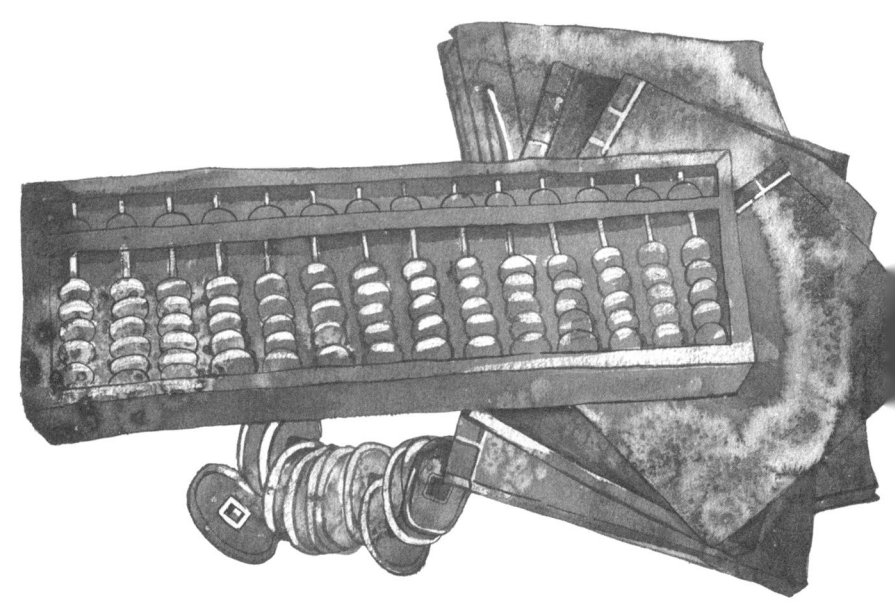

英韵《弟子规》

墨磨偏，

心不端，

字不敬，

心先病。

Ink going awry,
An unsteady eye;
Writing going apart,
An ill heart.

如果心不在焉，墨就会磨偏了，写出来的字就会歪歪斜斜。浮躁不安，心定不下来，是学不好的。

If you are absent-minded, your ink may go awry, and you cannot write well. So scatterbrained, you can never learn well.

列典籍,

有定处。

读看毕,

还原处。

Classics you list;
Know the gist.
Return the book
Where you took.

经典书籍应有顺序地阅读,了解其意旨。书籍诵读完毕须归还原处。

You should list the classics and read them in order to know what they mean. When you have read a book, return it to its original place.

虽有急，

卷束齐。

有缺坏，

就补之。

No matter how,
Books tidy enow.
Make up those
That you lose.

不管是什么情况，不论有多急，都要把书本收好。书本如有缺损就要修补，保持完整。

> Whatever the situation is or however you are, you should keep your books tidy. If your book is marred, you should repair it, making up those that you lose.

非圣书,
屏勿视。
蔽聪明,
坏心志。

Throw to nooks
The bad books.
If wickedly smart,
Rots your heart.

不是传述圣贤言行的著作,以及有害身心健康的不良书刊,都应该摒弃,以免身心受到污染,遭受蒙蔽。

If they are not saintly books or if they are injurious bad books, you should not read them. You should throw them away in case you are contaminated or misled.

勿自暴，

勿自弃。

圣与贤，

可驯致。

Try your best,
And never rest.
You seek, then,
The best men!

遇到困难或挫折的时候，不要自暴自弃，应该发奋向上，努力学习。不要忘记追求，圣贤境界虽高，只要持之以恒，也是可以达到的。

You should try your best to learn, and never rest even if in adverse conditions. And you should never forget your pursuit. You can catch up with the best men if you seek them and keep going toward the goal.

附录：
《弟子规》全文（汉语拼音版）

Canons for Disciples (Pinyin Version)

弟子规，圣人训。
首孝悌，次谨信。
泛爱众，而亲仁。
有余力，则学文。

入 则 孝

父母呼，应勿缓。
父母命，行勿懒。
父母教，须敬听。
父母责，须顺承。
冬则温，夏则凊。
晨则省，昏则定。
出必告，反必面。
居有常，业无变。
事虽小，勿擅为。
苟擅为，子道亏。
物虽小，勿私藏。
苟私藏，亲心伤。
亲所好，力为具。
亲所恶，谨为去。
身有伤，贻亲忧。
德有伤，贻亲羞。

亲爱我，孝何难。
亲恶我，孝方贤。
亲有过，谏使更。
怡吾色，柔吾声。
谏不入，悦复谏。
号泣随，挞无怨。
亲有疾，药先尝。
昼夜侍，不离床。
丧三年，常悲咽。
居处变，酒肉绝。
丧尽礼，祭尽诚。
事死者，如事生。

出则悌

兄道友，弟道恭。
兄弟睦，孝在中。
财物轻，怨何生。
言语忍，忿自泯。
或饮食，或坐走。
长者先，幼者后。
长呼人，即代叫。
人不在，己即到。

称尊长，勿呼名。
对尊长，勿见能。
路遇长，疾趋揖。
长无言，退恭立。
骑下马，乘下车。
过犹待，百步余。
长者立，幼勿坐。
长者坐，命乃坐。
尊长前，声要低。
低不闻，却非宜。
进必趋，退必迟。
问起对，视勿移。
事诸父，如事父。
事诸兄，如事兄。

谨

朝起早，夜眠迟。
老易至，惜此时。
晨必盥，兼漱口。
便溺回，辄净手。
冠必正，纽必结。
袜与履，俱紧切。

zhì guān fú　yǒu dìng wèi
置冠服，有定位。
wù luàn dùn　zhì wū huì
勿乱顿，致污秽。
yī guì jié　bú guì huá
衣贵洁，不贵华。
shàng xún fèn　xià chèn jiā
上循分，下称家。
duì yǐn shí　wù jiǎn zé
对饮食，勿拣择。
shí shì kě　wù guò zé
食适可，勿过则。
nián fāng shào　wù yǐn jiǔ
年方少，勿饮酒。
yǐn jiǔ zuì　zuì wéi chǒu
饮酒醉，最为丑。
bù cóng róng　lì duān zhèng
步从容，立端正。
yī shēn yuán　bài gōng jìng
揖深圆，拜恭敬。
wù jiàn yù　wù bǒ yǐ
勿践阈，勿跛倚。
wù jī jù　wù yáo bì
勿箕踞，勿摇髀。
huǎn jiē lián　wù yǒu shēng
缓揭帘，勿有声。
kuān zhuǎn wān　wù chù léng
宽转弯，勿触棱。
zhí xū qì　rú zhí yíng
执虚器，如执盈。
rù xū shì　rú yǒu rén
入虚室，如有人。
shì wù máng　máng duō cuò
事勿忙，忙多错。
wù wèi nán　wù qīng lüè
勿畏难，勿轻略。
dòu nào chǎng　jué wù jìn
斗闹场，绝勿近。
xié pì shì　jué wù wèn
邪僻事，绝勿问。
jiāng rù mén　wèn shú cún
将入门，问孰存。
jiāng shàng táng　shēng bì yáng
将上堂，声必扬。
rén wèn shuí　duì yǐ míng
人问谁，对以名。

吾与我，不分明。
用人物，须明求。
倘不问，即为偷。
借人物，及时还。
人借物，有勿悭。

信

凡出言，信为先。
诈与妄，奚可焉。
话说多，不如少。
惟其是，勿佞巧。
奸巧语，秽污词。
市井气，切戒之。
见未真，勿轻言。
知未的，勿轻传。
事非宜，勿轻诺。
苟轻诺，进退错。
凡道字，重且舒。
勿急疾，勿模糊。
彼说长，此说短。
不关己，莫闲管。
见人善，即思齐。

zòng qù yuǎn　yǐ jiàn jī
纵去远，以渐跻。
jiàn rén è　jí nèi xǐng
见人恶，即内省。
yǒu zé gǎi　wú jiā jǐng
有则改，无加警。
wéi dé xué　wéi cái yì
唯德学，唯才艺。
bù rú rén　dāng zì lì
不如人，当自砺。
ruò yī fu　ruò yǐn shí
若衣服，若饮食。
bù rú rén　wù shēng qī
不如人，勿生戚。
wén guò nù　wén yù lè
闻过怒，闻誉乐。
sǔn yǒu lái　yì yǒu què
损友来，益友却。
wén yù kǒng　wén guò xīn
闻誉恐，闻过欣。
zhí liàng shì　jiàn xiāng qīn
直谅士，渐相亲。
wú xīn fēi　míng wéi cuò
无心非，名为错。
yǒu xīn fēi　míng wéi è
有心非，名为恶。
guò néng gǎi　guī yú wú
过能改，归于无。
tǎng yǎn shì　zēng yì gū
倘掩饰，增一辜。

fàn ài zhòng　泛爱众

fán shì rén　jiē xū ài
凡是人，皆须爱。
tiān tóng fù　dì tóng zài
天同覆，地同载。
xíng gāo zhě　míng zì gāo
行高者，名自高。
rén suǒ zhòng　fēi mào gāo
人所重，非貌高。
cái dà zhě　wàng zì dà
才大者，望自大。

人所服，非言大。
己有能，勿自私。
人所能，勿轻訾。
勿谄富，勿骄贫。
勿厌故，勿喜新。
人不闲，勿事搅。
人不安，勿话扰。
人有短，切莫揭。
人有私，切莫说。
道人善，即是善。
人知之，愈思勉。
扬人恶，即是恶。
疾之甚，祸且作。
善相劝，德皆建。
过不规，道两亏。
凡取与，贵分晓。
与宜多，取宜少。
将加人，先问己。
己不欲，即速已。
恩欲报，怨欲忘。
抱怨短，报恩长。
待婢仆，身贵端。
虽贵端，慈而宽。

shì fú rén　xīn bù rán
势服人，心不然。
lǐ fú rén　fāng wú yán
理服人，方无言。

亲　仁
qīn　rén

tóng shì rén　lèi bù qí
同是人，类不齐。
liú sú zhòng　rén zhě xī
流俗众，仁者稀。
guǒ rén zhě　rén duō wèi
果仁者，人多畏。
yán bú huì　sè bú mèi
言不讳，色不媚。
néng qīn rén　wú xiàn hǎo
能亲仁，无限好。
dé rì jìn　guò rì shǎo
德日进，过日少。
bù qīn rén　wú xiàn hài
不亲仁，无限害。
xiǎo rén jìn　bǎi shì huài
小人进，百事坏。

余 力 学 文
yú　lì　xué　wén

bú lì xíng　dàn xué wén
不力行，但学文。
zhǎng fú huá　chéng hé rén
长浮华，成何人。
dàn lì xíng　bù xué wén
但力行，不学文。
rèn jǐ jiàn　mèi lǐ zhēn
任己见，昧理真。
dú shū fǎ　yǒu sān dào
读书法，有三到。
xīn yǎn kǒu　xìn jiē yào
心眼口，信皆要。
fāng dú cǐ　wù mù bǐ
方读此，勿慕彼。

此未终，彼勿起。
宽为限，紧用功。
工夫到，滞塞通。
心有疑，随札记。
就人问，求确义。
房室清，墙壁净。
几案洁，笔砚正。
墨磨偏，心不端。
字不敬，心先病。
列典籍，有定处。
读看毕，还原处。
虽有急，卷束齐。
有缺坏，就补之。
非圣书，屏勿视。
蔽聪明，坏心志。
勿自暴，勿自弃。
圣与贤，可驯致。

跋

外语界大都知道我是做语言学的。常有人问我：怎么做起了经典英译？此事起于两次偶然。1985年大学毕业后的九年间，由于受"知识无用"和"下海浪潮"的冲击，我除了教材和信件之外就没有读过任何东西了。我教过的理工科博士生毕业后很快就做了教授、处长，还有一位做了副校长，在学术和事业上突飞猛进。而我突然发现自己远远地落后了，曾经的自负青年已经迷失了方向，仿佛要被时代抛弃，被学界抛弃了。为了起死回生的一线希望，我到新华书店翻翻书，看看能从哪方面发现一丝做学问的线索。我找到一本汉语成语英译的书。我觉得英译不需要什么理论，有点语言功夫就行，于是就买了一本汉语成语。回到家试译，竟然有诗的感觉。后来又发现有人还译过古诗，我很好奇，试译一两首后便发现译诗很上手，心里很激动。从1994年开始我译了一年多，写满了四本日记本，约有几百首古典诗词，其中包括《诗经》中的《国风》部分。调到广外后我开始接触语言学，就无暇顾及译诗了。此后大约十五年，就再没有译过诗。第二次偶然，是我要调到天津外国语大学的时候。那是2011年的夏天，我满脑子还都是语言学、形式之类的玄思。在宾馆午休时，突然间脑子中冒出译《三字经》的念头。如果译成英语，"三字"该如何处理呢？能否以三个英语单词对译汉语的三个字呢？这是我"形式"的习惯性思维。在常人看来这根本不可能，但我很快译出了第一节，而且用了偶韵，于是拟定三词格偶韵体的模板——采用韵律是原文的要求也是诗学的要求。翻译的过程很愉快，两天半就译完了！

第一次偶然是穷途末路的偶遇，第二次偶然是"形式"这一学科意识的触发。

英译完《英韵〈三字经〉》之后我才得知西方译家早就翻译过《三字经》了，而且有十多个译本。

世界上最早的《三字经》译本是利玛窦的老师罗明坚首译的拉丁语译本。而后，西方相继出现了多种英文译本，如英国人马礼逊的、美国传教士裨治文的，等等。但这些译者都只是对诗文进行散文化的解释，更无法满足"三字"这一形式的要求。纵观中西方译家，哪一位还原了中国文学的"是其所是"了呢？英语的《千字文》还是《千字文》吗？《十六字令》《长相思》呢？海量的唐、宋诗词呢？新近翻了翻宇文所安译的《杜甫诗》，这也都是散文化的解释。

如果说译文扭曲、变形，这不难理解。在字数固定的特定文本框架内翻译古诗几乎是不可能的——《三字经》就曾被西方翻译家视为天使不敢涉足的地方。那么中国哲学译成外文又如何呢？黑格尔、洪堡特、德里达等都说中国没有哲学，没有演绎逻辑等等。他们凭什么如此论断？他们懂汉语吗？如果不懂汉语，那读谁翻译的文献而得出这样的结论呢？哲学文本虽然少有诗体的制约，但要传达它的是其所是，也绝非易事。我猛然认识到：中国文化被曲解了，其价值被低估了，其神采被遮蔽了。

至此我隐约感到了使命的召唤！

基于我对中西哲学的理解，要跨越语言的天堑，如不上升到语言和翻译的形而上学，不深入到它们的肌理，要做好经典翻译是绝对不可能的。我杂食动物的天性也成了优势。我系统思考过神学、哲学、逻辑、语言、文学以及翻译学本身，基于此便在翻译中确立了悖论性的两条原则：不可违反的刚性原则和无时不变的柔性原则，而在"易"的过程中求诸化矛盾为不矛盾的可拓逻辑，以类比（analogy）的方式找到相似点，在"字""词"或"音步"之间建立类比关系，在形式和意义的张力之间和种种矛盾之中找到最佳平衡点。

在2011年以后的大部分时间里我转向了经史子集的英译，开始了"以诗译诗、以经译经"的奥德赛之旅。

翻译的过程总的来说十分愉快，常有一气呵成的时候，激动得睡不着觉。

苦思冥想的时候也是有的。主要是古代文献时代太久，找不到注解、阐释，也不好考证。

常有人问我翻译的时候会参考前人的翻译吗？我说：不！我主要想保持判断的独立性，也怕被错误的认识所误导。即便是经典原文的汉语解释，我也保持高度的警惕性。对于难解的地方我会求诸词源或句法分析，然后再找文献印证。比如，我把"道"译为"Word"是因为《道德经》的"道"、《圣经》的"Word"和赫拉克利特的《论自然》的"Logos"都是万物的本原。中西经典在以不同的方式叙述同样的故事："道生万物"或"道成肉身"。"word"本义是"生殖器"，转喻为"生"，所以以"Word"对译"道"可以融通中西本体论哲学。而且"道可道非常道"译作"The Word that can be worded is not the Word *per se*"不仅语义上契合，而且也与原文"道"这一关键词的异质同构的复现和跌宕形成照应。相比之下，"The Tao that can be trodden is not the enduring and unchanging Tao""The Way that can be told of is not an Unvarying Way"之类是不是有些问题？经典翻译中陷阱很多，根据字面来理解远远不够，还要靠逻辑和语篇来推导，比如"道常无名"通常的解释是"道永远是无名的"。这显然是违背常识和《道德经》的精神的：没有"名"就无法言说。其实"道"就是"道"的名字，而且它也有别名，如"谷神""天下母""玄牝之门"等。为何是这种语序呢？这正是汉语的一种结构，即否定词插入名词或名词词组之间。"道常无名"实际上就相当于"道无常名"。你可以对比"菩提本无树"（本无菩提树）和现代汉语的"知不道"（不知道），其句法和语义的关系不就很清楚了吗？那么汉语为何采用这种结构呢？如果纵览先验知识和后验知识以及人类语言的结构就不难理解了——这便通向了形而上学，而这又验证了《道德经》跨越时空的真理性。译完"道常无名"，我想如果我的理解是对的，历史上必然会有人和我理解一样。所幸，我找到了《道德经》河上公最早的阐释："道能阴能阳，能弛能张，能存能亡，故无常名也。"看来河上公是完全同意我的观点的。

许多朋友经常问我翻译的秘诀。哪有什么秘诀？不过就是守住"是其所是"的杂学的综合应用。首先要以翻译本身为立足点探究何为翻译；其次将翻译本体论、翻译机制和语言表征性进行综合把握；再其次就是文史哲知识了。就语言学知识而言，需要具备语法、语义、语用、语篇诸层次的知识；就文学而言，需要具有押韵、韵式、节奏、音步以及审美构成、文学性生成机制等方面的知识；就历史而言，需要了解当时的文明形态和体制、事件等；就哲学而言，需要体悟中西本体论、认识论、方法论、价值论的异同。译者的知识是杂——既要博又要专。

由于巨大的语言差异，做到形神兼备、圆满调和，的确不容易。然而，为了再现中华元素和保全文本自身的价值，作为译者我们只能孜孜以求了。

Afterword

The foreign language teaching world all know I do linguistics. Some friends often wonder why I'm now doing classic translation. This I can trace back to two accidents. In the nine years after my college graduation in 1985, I didn't read any except letters and textbooks, so influenced by "no use for scholars' work" and "going-for-business craze". The science and engineering PhD students I taught rushed to power soon after their graduation: professors, deans, and one of them became a vice president. I was left to realize I was lagging far behind, deserted by the age and the academic world —the once ambitious young man was lost. For a possible ray of hope to come back to life, I went to a Xinhua bookstore to cast a glance over books, to see if I could find some clues to learning. I found a book of idiom translation. I felt English translation need no much theory, just some command of language, so I bought a book of Chinese idioms. I tried translating some and felt an impulse of poetry. Later, I came to find some verse translations and was very curious and tried translating a few poems. "That's it", I found myself good at it. From 1994, I translated classic poems for about one year, filling four note books with a few hundred translations, including *The Airs of the States* from *The Book of Songs*. When I moved to Guangdong Foreign Studies University, I got obsessed with linguistics, no more time to spend on translation. For about 15 years, I had never translated any. The second accident was when I moved to Tianjin Foreign Studies University. It was the summer of 2011, when I was buried deep in linguistics, form in particular. When I was about to have a nap, *Sanzi Jing* (*Three Character Book* interlinearly) occurred to me. If translated into English, how would 'three character' be done with? What about translating three characters into three words? This is a matter of form. In many people's eyes, it would be impossible, but I finished the first stanza very soon, three words a line, two lines in couplets. Then I decided on the three-word-a-line-couplet template. The rhyme is what is required by the original and by prosody. I felt very happy about it and finished the book in two and a half days.

The first accident was one in a cul-de-sac; the second accident was one triggered by form.

Only after I finished *Three Word Primer in English Rhyme* did I come to know western translators had translated the classic, more than ten versions actually. The first one was a Latin version by Michele Ruggieri, followed by versions of Morrison, Bridgman, and so on. But theirs are but interpretations of the original, having failed to represent the form of "three words a line" and "rhyme". If you look back at all previous translators, who has rendered Chinese literature as it is? Is an English translation of *One Thousand Characters* (*Qian Zi Wen*) still *One Thousand Characters*? Sixteen Character lyrics? Long Longing? And an ocean of Tang and Song Poems? Recently, I have had a look at Stephen Owen's translation of *The Poetry of Du Fu*. The poetry has become prose.

If you say a translation may be a twisted or warped version, you are right in most cases, because it is impossible to finish a translation of a certain text type within strict constraints of definite words a line—Translating *Three Character Book* has been regarded as something angels dare not tread on. What about Chinese philosophy translated into western languages? Hegel, Humboldt, Derrida and many others have asserted that Chinese have no philosophy or deduction. Where are their evidences? Did or do they know Chinese? If not, whose translations have they read to come to such a conclusion? Though philosophy is not usually constrained by prosody or scansion, it is not at all easy to render it as it is.

Now I've suddenly awakened: Chinese culture has been misunderstood, devalued or eclipsed.

I seem to have heard a call of mission!

As far as I know based on my knowledge of philosophy, it is absolutely impossible to break through the barriers between languages to do classic translation well if one is not risen to the metaphysics of language and translation while buried in the depth of their mechanism. My omnivorous nature has been an advantage. I have explored into theology, philosophy, logic, language, literature and translation itself, and have set up two paradoxical principles for translation: the principle of rigidity that one should not violate and the principle of fluidity with which one can change elements of a text anytime and anywhere. Abiding by the principles, one should take resort to extenic logic that can turn contradictions into non-contradictions, and find similarities by analogy between characters and words or syllables or between rhythms and rhymes in the different languages and keep the best possible balance between all contradictions.

After 2011, I turned to translation of Chinese classics, hence the Odyssey of translating Poesie into Poesie and Classic into Classic.

The process of translation can be euphoric. Sometimes I feel I can finish something at one breath, and sometimes I feel too excited to fall asleep.

And there are occasions for brain cudgeling ruminations. Many ancient literatures are too old to understand or analyze.

I'm often asked whether I make reference to previous translations when doing mine. My answer is No. I want to be independent, afraid of being misled. I even keep guard against annotations done by Chinese scholars. In face of puzzles, I will trace to etymology or have a syntactic analysis and then try to find proofs. For example, I translated "Dao" into "Word" because "Dao" in *Daode Jing*, "Word" in *The Bible* and "Logos" in *Physis* are the same ontic being or the primal force of the universe. These books tell the same story in different ways: The Word begets everything, or it can be termed as reincarnation. The original meaning of "word" is "sexual organ", having extended to "give birth to" through metaphor. So the translation of "Dao" into "Word" can be seen as having fused eastern and western ontological philosophies. And the English translation of "The Word that can be worded is not the Word *per se*" from "Dao ke dao fei chang dao" is not only correspondent in semantics but also the same in rhetoric and style—the isomorphic repetition and rhythm. In contrast, problems are prevalent in such versions as "The Tao that can be trodden is not the enduring and unchanging Tao" and "The Way that can be told of is not an Unvarying Way". There are many traps in classic translation. Interpretation based on linear word order is far from enough; you have to make an inference based on logic and textuality, for example, "Dao chang wu ming" (interlinearly: Word constant not have name) is explained as "Dao has no name for ever". This is obviously nonsensical, against the spirit of *Daode Jing*, because without a name nothing is sayable. Actually, Dao is the name of Dao, and it has other names such as Gu Shen (Vale Spirit), Mother of the World, and Gate of Virgin Fair and so on. Then, why this word order? This is actually a syntactic structure of Chinese, that is, the negative operator is inserted in the noun or nominal phrase; it is an alternative of "Dao wu chang ming (interlinearly: Word not have constant name; translation: The Word has no constant name)". If you compare this with "pu ti ben wu shu (interlinearly: Bodhi not have tree; translation: There is no Budhi tree.)" or "wo zhi bu dao (interlinearly: I have i-no-dea; translation: I have no idea)", you will know the structure and semantics. Why is there such a structure in Chinese? It is easy to understand if you have a distinction and integration of a priori and a posteriori knowledge—This leads to metaphysics and this testifies to the universal truth and value of *Daode Jing* (*The World and the World*). Having solved this, I thought if I was right, there must be someone having the same understanding as I. Luckily, I found the earliest explanation by Lord River: "The Word can shift between Shade and Shine, between contraction and relaxation, between life and death, hence no constant name." Lord River agreed with me.

Many friends have asked me the knack for good translation. This is actually a comprehensive application of a hodgepodge of everything while keeping A=A (Whatever is, is). First, translation itself should be emphasized; second, one needs to have an integral understanding of its ontological status, mechanism and the representation of language, and then one should have a good command of literary, historical and philosophical knowledge. In terms of linguistics, one needs to have syntactic, semantic, pragmatic and discourse perspectives;

in terms of literature, one needs to have such knowledge as rhyme, rhyming scheme, rhythm, meter as well as aesthetic composition, the mechanism of literary creation and so on; in terms of history one needs to know civilization, institutionalization and events that a work may have to do; in terms of philosophy, one needs to have a good apprehension of the similarities and differences between eastern and western ontology, epistemology, methodology and axiology. A good translator needs to know everything of something and something of everything.

Constrained by the vast differences between source and target languages, it is not at all easy to do a good and well-tuned translation with the proper tension between form and meaning. But to represent what is idiosyncratically Chinese and retain the value of a text itself, a translator has no alternative.

作者简介

赵 彦 春

上海大学教授,北京语言大学、中山大学、中国农业大学、天津科技大学、天津财经大学等高校兼职教授或者客座教授,印度Mericet大学学术委员会委员,国际东西方学会学术委员会委员,国际学术期刊 *Translating China* 主编,台湾政治大学《广译》编委,国际汉学与教育研究会会长,国学双语研究会执行会长,中国语言教育研究会副会长。涉猎哲学、语言学、翻译学等多门专业,在哲学、语言、文学等领域,发表科研论文近百篇,出版专著8部、译著19部,编审教材和主编教材20多部,主持国家社科基金重点项目、国家新闻出版署重点规划项目以及省部级重点课题等7项。翻译实践上坚守以诗译诗、以经译经的准则。2017年出版的《英韵〈三字经〉》是有史以来第一部以三个英语单词对应三个汉字的偶韵体《三字经》译文,被新华社、人民日报、光明日报、中国日报、中央电视台、二十一世纪英文报、渤海日报、今晚报、天津广播电台以及今日头条、网易等国内外各大知名媒体的广泛报道，被誉为"有史以来最美汉英翻译""神翻译""神还原"。

About the Author

Zhao Yan-chun is Professor of English at Shanghai University and Guest Professor at Beijing Language and Culture University, Sun Yat-sen University, Beijing Agriculture University and many other universities. He is President of International Sinology and Education, President of Chinese Classics Bilinguals' Association, Vice President of Language Education Association of China, Research Fellow of the International Association for East-West Studies, Member of Academic Committee of Mericet, India, Member of the Academic Committee of the International Society of East and West, Editor of *Translating China*, and Editorial Board Member of *Guangyi* in Taiwan National Chengchi University. His academic interests include translation studies, linguistics and philosophy. He has written extensively about the relationship between philosophy, language, literature and translation and has published about 100 academic papers, 8 monographs and 19 classic translations and more than 20 text books, and has chaired and undertaken 7 national and provincial key projects, including one sponsored by the National Social Science Fund and one sponsored by the State Administration of Press, Publication, Radio, Film and Television. He adheres to the principle of translating Poesie into Poesie and Classic into Classic. His *Three Word Primer in English Rhyme* (2017) has been widely reported by international, national and local media such as *People's Daily*, *China Daily*, CCTV, acclaimed as the unprecedented Chinese-English translation, the best, the choice, the cream.

图书在版编目（CIP）数据

英韵《弟子规》= Canons for Disciples in English Rhyme／赵彦春译注. -- 北京：高等教育出版社，2018.10

（赵彦春国学经典英译系列）

ISBN 978-7-04-049649-9

Ⅰ.①英… Ⅱ.①赵… Ⅲ.①古汉语-启蒙读物-英文 Ⅳ.①H194.1

中国版本图书馆CIP数据核字(2018)第083672号

英韵《弟子规》
Yingyun Dizigui

策划编辑	徐莉萍　洪世英
责任编辑	徐莉萍　洪世英
书籍设计	刘晓翔
责任校对	张　薇
插图绘制	王　静
责任印制	韩　刚
出版发行	高等教育出版社
社址	北京市西城区德外大街4号
邮政编码	100120
购书热线	010-58581118
咨询电话	400-810-0598
网址	http://www.hep.edu.cn
	http://www.hep.com.cn
网上订购	http://www.hepmall.com.cn
	http://www.hepmall.com
	http://www.hepmall.cn
印刷	北京雅昌艺术印刷有限公司
开本	787mm×960mm 1/16
印张	11.5
字数	110千字
版次	2018年10月第1版
印次	2018年10月第1次印刷
定价	68.00元

本书如有缺页、倒页、脱页等质量问题，请到所购图书销售部门联系调换
版权所有　侵权必究
物料号　49649-00

郑重声明——高等教育出版社依法对本书享有专有出版权。任何未经许可的复制、销售行为均违反《中华人民共和国著作权法》，其行为人将承担相应的民事责任和行政责任；构成犯罪的，将被依法追究刑事责任。为了维护市场秩序，保护读者的合法权益，避免读者误用盗版书造成不良后果，我社将配合行政执法部门和司法机关对违法犯罪的单位和个人进行严厉打击。社会各界人士如发现上述侵权行为，希望及时举报，本社将奖励举报有功人员。

反盗版举报电话
（010）58581999　58582371　58582488
反盗版举报传真
（010）82086060
反盗版举报邮箱
dd@hep.com.cn
通信地址
北京市西城区德外大街 4 号
高等教育出版社法律事务与版权管理部
邮政编码
100120